Unveilir
of Being ... Much

# Finally
## *Taking Up*
# Space

Shana V. Hartman & Cindy Urbanski, Editors

SYNERGY
PUBLISHING GROUP

BELMONT, NORTH CAROLINA

*Unveiling the Secrets of Being Too Much: Finally Taking Up Space*
Shana V. Hartman & Cindy Urbanski, Editors

Published by Synergy Publishing Group, Belmont, NC
Cover and interior by Melisa Graham

Softcover ISBN 978-1-960892-25-6
E-book ISBN 978-1-960892-26-3

Synergy Publishing Group Mission Statement: A Dedication

We envision a world where all voices are heard and all experiences are valued. We believe writing is a pathway to connecting with self and honoring our experiences. We encourage the sharing of our voices with the world because we believe it promotes community connections and collective healing. Through embodied writing experiences, Synergy Publishing Group guides and supports writers, scribblers, and storytellers on their unique journeys to leave a legacy with their words.

We dedicate this book to those writers, scribblers, and storytellers who are committed to leaving a legacy with their words.

# Contents

*Introduction:*

# Faerie. Not Fairy.

---

## Cindy Urbanski

---

I desperately wanted to include "spreading faerie dust" in the title of the book you are holding. *Faerie*, not *fairy*. Think more Celtic goddesses and less Tinkerbell. Beautiful, ethereal, wise, mischievous, sensual. This is the kind of "dust" we are scattering about in the pages before you. But, as Shana and I discussed the amazing pieces in this volume, we realized the faerie dust is actually on the inside! So I am using this powerful word here as a way in for you, dear reader. Let me explain!

Since publishing *Unveiling the Secrets: An Encyclopedia for Women and Those Who Love Them* in 2023, Shana and I, along with the other goddess types who contributed their wisdom and words in that book, have been talking with people who have their own secrets to share. And through those discussions, we discovered that we all had more to share. Hence, the birth of the *Unveiling the Secrets* SERIES! Yep. That's in all caps with an exclamation point because, holy cow, who knew we would be doing a series of books?!

Like we often do around here at Synergy Publishing Group, we threw the proverbial spaghetti at the wall to see what stuck with what we initially called a "wild card" book. What stuck were bits of faerie dust. This collection is vast in its expanse and, as the title proclaims, is about taking up space in a world where marginalized groups are often taught to play small and stay quiet. As our mission statement proclaims, "We encourage the sharing of our voices with the world because we believe it promotes community connections and collective healing." There is something for everyone here. I am tempted to do a rundown, but that's what the table of contents is for. What I *will* say is that each of these pieces could be the topic for its own *Unveiling the Secrets* book. Each author, each story, each experience, each space-claiming tale is a jumping-off point for even more inspiration and stories to come, just like our first *Unveiling the Secrets* book inspired us to keep going and create the book you are holding now.

So ... I invite you not only to read and relish each piece found here, but also to let your mind wander to what you might have to say about each of the topics explored in these pieces. Then take a chance, fill out our submission form, and potentially become a published author in one of the next books in the *Unveiling the Secrets* series. Become a part of this powerful community of faerie secret-tellers. I promise your words will matter deeply to someone. Shana will be back at the end to tell you how.

# Our Writerly Coven

---

## Melisa Graham

---

We gather here deliberately to breathe
inhaling the invincible forces of creation
exhaling the delusions that we are less
our intentions echo through all the worlds
our thoughts so powerful they sound in each ear
like music floating on a healing breeze
rippling and swirling
through the depths of earth and water
through the heights of air and fire
through shadow and light
disconnecting us from our personas
birthing new connections to our truest selves
sewing a valuable tapestry of souls
united in radical vulnerability and expression
come calm, come chaos
come bounty, come lack
no external force can tear these threads
we allow only new lived experiences
like new colors bursting across the warp
as we will it, so shall it be

# Pointing

## Melisa Graham

A room full of women and one man gathered in a rough circle on our last day together as a group. The past few days had been a nonstop exchange of ideas, feedback, and wringing the words from our brains onto each person's writing medium of choice. In moments of rest at this embodied writing retreat, we had stared at a gaggle of geese, a lone white squirrel, or ripples on the lake. Or we'd gathered around the kitchen island nibbling the various snacks Cindy, our own personal chef de cuisine, had laid out for us.

Once in our rough circle, Shana did as Shana does and invited us to close our eyes, breathe, and ground ourselves in the moment. Then Cindy introduced an exercise called *pointing*. Before the explanation, I'd imagined fingers pointed in my face with cries of *j'accuse* echoing around me. That was just my inner stress bunny making up stories though; I needn't have worried. In the real world, we'd each read a few sentences or a paragraph from something we'd written that day, and then the others would say two words that stuck with them from the reading. So *pointing* in this case meant *highlighting, reflecting, echoing,* or *amplifying.* (I vote for a name change.)

Before the exercise began, I got the feeling I needed to record it, that we needed to do something with these echoed words and feelings. I asked the group's permission and set my phone in the center of the room. The words that emerged ... *calm, chaos, invincible, persona, powerful, delusion, sewing, music, breathe, sound, radical, healing* ... gradually formed a picture in my head, independent of each reading but very much tied to my feelings about this group of people and our time together.

The day after the retreat, some of us gathered again online for our bimonthly writing group. I pulled out the recording of our pointing exercise, transcribed the words, and described the picture they'd formed in my head. And thus, "Our Writerly Coven" was written with a piece of each person from the retreat fused in free verse. You will find essays from many of them within this book.

I should note (for those averse to the notion) that no actual witchcraft was performed at this writing retreat—unless you count breathing deeply into one's intentions, drinking herbal teas, communing with nature, gathering two or more women unrelated by blood, having one or more moles or distinguishing scars on one's body, mumbling to oneself while working out a troubling bit of wordsmithing, being stubborn, or being old—all of which, in darker times, could have led to a woman's execution. If you believe any of those things qualify as magic or you otherwise subscribe to the tenets of the *Malleus Maleficarum*, then indeed much witchcraft occurred.

# Live the Questions

## Melisa Graham

I like answers. They're like the period at the end of a sentence: quantifiable, finite, direct. With a pocketful of great answers, I know my place and can map my path. But life doesn't always have great answers, so then what? Well, then, if you're lucky, you meet someone who gives you a new map.

I got such a map from a man named Lightning Brown who visited one of my college classes. My professor, Reynolds Price, occasionally invited guests to the class, where we were studying his personal translation of the gospels of Mark and John and exploring the apocryphal gospels. One time, the guest was James Taylor. I was late for class and missed the introductions, and the only photo I'd ever seen of him was from the '70s. Based on his commentary about music and religion, I spent the whole class thinking he was a music professor.

Lightning Brown introduced himself as a "Catholic Buddhist." I didn't know what that meant, but I fell in love with him immediately. Not romantic love, of course, but the kind of love that makes you want to kiss and hug someone's brain, that makes you want to sit at their feet and drink in every word that falls from their mouths and pens. His name alone was word candy, and then he introduced himself with blasphemy! I would henceforth follow this man wherever he led me.

Professor Price was having us share snippets from our primary writing assignment—an original apocryphal gospel. After I read my snippet,

Mr. Brown said, "Your writing reminds me of Rainer Maria Rilke. Are you familiar with him?" At the time, I wasn't. Good thing, or I might have burst out crying in front of my fellow students, whom I found intellectually intimidating on my best day.

After class, I immediately went to the campus bookstore and bought *The Selected Poetry of Rainer Maria Rilke* translated by Stephen Mitchell. That copy is now stained and tattered, like any well-worn map. I will confess that I dog-ear pages to mark my spot or places I want to revisit. That book is now full of little love triangles, places I return again and again for inspiration.

Later, I got a copy of *Letters to a Young Poet*, and it became my first mentor, encouraging me to write even if just for myself because I must. And one day, this book gave me more than just a map—it gave me a new guiding star.

It was the sort of day when no answers were forthcoming. Instead, a thousand questions were swirling around me, slicing and sucking little bits of me away into the whirlwind. *Was my relationship failing? Was I loved? Was God real? What did I believe? What does "faith" even mean? What was the point of this existence? What should I do with the rest of my life? What had I done to deserve this life?*

I pulled out *Letters to a Young Poet*, either to distract myself or to find an answer, and found Rilke's advice to soothe my swirling mind: "Be patient toward all that is unsolved in your heart and try to love the questions themselves like locked rooms and like books that are written in a very foreign tongue. Do not now seek the answers, which cannot be given you because you would not be able to live them. And the point is, to live everything. Live the questions now. Perhaps you will then gradually, without noticing it, live along some distant day into the answer."[1]

I took a deep breath, let the questions settle, and turned my face to the sun.

Rilke has his critics, of course—those who say he was a hypocrite, a sycophantic worshiper of the upper class, an opportunist, and a con man

---

1   This translation by M.D. Herter Norton (W.W. Norton & Company, 2004).

whose poetry is too abstract. After reading the criticism, I had to wonder if Mr. Brown had complimented or insulted me. I chose, ultimately, to take it as a compliment and to separate my love for Rilke's writing from my feelings about the man. Such is the way in our modern world where role models rarely withstand scrutiny.

I can't claim to have lived all the questions or figured out all the answers, even though thirty years have passed since that day. Some things take time, a whole lifetime even as we gather bits and pieces of understanding along the way. Even once we understand something, we may forget and find ourselves once again living the question. And that's okay. Questions are the beautiful curves along the scenic route.

---

MELISA GRAHAM is a writer, editor, designer, and publishing consultant who works primarily with independent authors and publishers. Her superpower is helping storytellers look like professional writers, and she is happiest when her work involves interesting people, ideas, solutions, and stories. Her writing has appeared in *Kakalak 2013*, *626 TRIBE* magazine, the *Unveiling the Secrets* anthology series, and her small collection of poetry, *Used Cow for Sale*. Connect with Melisa on LinkedIn and Instagram @1smelisa or on her website at melisagrahamcreative.com.

# I Want to Know What Love Is:

## A Parable in Three Acts

---

### Rachel C. Patterson

---

## Prelude

I have always wanted to know what true love is. Yet, in most of my relationships, I've always felt like a piece of me was missing. Not feeling whole and seeing couples walking hand and hand looking into each other's eyes, I could tell there was a strong connection that I didn't have.

It wasn't until I got divorced that I truly began to understand the idea of love. Why? When I got divorced, I went on a journey to heal and help me find a healthier me. I felt all the feelings I didn't want: abandonment, loneliness, anger, and frustration. The house felt so empty and cold. I could hear the echoes.

Yet, after my divorce, I found out I liked being alone in spite of wanting to be married. Because I didn't have to walk around wondering what was going to happen next. I wasn't expected to cook a meal for anyone. I could just pour a bowl of cereal or have a sundae for dinner if I chose. But, on the other hand, I missed having someone by my side, someone to come home and talk to, besides my dog. During this transition from being married to being single, I asked myself what I could do to better myself.

One thing I could do was focus on my health. I heard energy healing work might help. I sat down by the computer and searched online for Reiki practitioners because I felt my energy was way off post-divorce. I found someone who practiced locally. When I called, we talked, but I realized I didn't need to say much. She knew exactly what I needed without me telling her. Without hesitation, I made an appointment to see her in person, and she began to help me heal.

On one of the visits with this particular Reiki master, she curiously asked me a question: "What does this mean to you: 'I want to know what love is?'" It was something that came to her while she was holding on to my head and shoulders. It was a song from the '80s band Foreigner. As I lay there on the massage table, warm and content under the blanket, looking up at her, I said, "It is just a song, and it doesn't have any meaning to me." For the life of me, I couldn't figure out why she thought of that song as she worked with me. It really puzzled me. However, after my session, I slowly started to make a connection to what she was asking me. I had to go back almost fifteen years from that moment on the table to begin to unwind what love meant to me.

## Act I: Meeting (Who I Thought Was) Mr. Right

This sales guy "waltzed" right into the salon I was working in at the time, and I mean waltzed right in like he owned the place, using his Southern charm. I was working on a client and had to stop. He was not your typical salesman, for he had on a brightly colored Western shirt. Later, that shirt would symbolize the disloyalty I would experience. All he was missing was the cowboy hat. He came in with the glamour picture proofs that we had taken of all of us in the salon a month prior.

He caught my attention, and I definitely caught his because he made an appointment for a manicure with me, so he could hold my hand and ask me out in a nonchalant way. He seemed to cast something powerful over me that I couldn't resist.

So we had our first date, and from then on he would travel back and forth, from wherever his job took him, to see me. Before I knew it, we were dating, and I went with him everywhere. I felt like I was traveling the world with him. We had such a great relationship in those early days, and I felt like I had all that I wanted. I was treated like I was his world.

## Act 2: Marriage Proposal (Among Many Things) Gone Wrong

My mom called one day while he and I were together watching a movie and asked when we were getting married. We had sort of talked about it once or twice, but nothing was ever serious. Putting the phone on my shoulder, I said, "Mom wants to know if we are getting married." His answer, "You know I want to marry you." And that was it! That was his proposal. I looked at him like a deer in headlights because this was not at all how I thought a loving marriage would start out, but since I felt like he was "the one," at the time, I just went with it.

So we began to prepare for our big day together. Financially, we lived mostly day to day, so there wasn't too much we could afford to put toward the wedding. Thankfully, my dad stepped in and bought the gown that made me feel like a princess. I absolutely said "yes" to this dress! I noticed the lovely lace that went down to a point on my hand, and it caught my attention that I still had a bare ring finger.

One thing I always dreamed about was having matching wedding bands. And we found the perfect matching set at a pawn shop. One thing about my fiancé I was thankful for was his ability to haggle and get things at cheaper prices. But this haggling and manipulative behavior would later be used against me to get what he wanted. I so desperately wanted to know what love was that I could not see some of these foreshadowing signs.

My then fiancé moved to South Carolina to live and work. When I called to see how things were going, I almost missed the chance to get my ring because he shared that he didn't have the money to pay the balance off. Thankfully, I used some wedding present cash we had received. We were all set for my fairytale wedding.

Our wedding was small, but great. We got married outside under a canopy of leaves and flowers in a beautiful location in upstate New York. We didn't have too much, but what we had, we made do. After the ceremony, my cheeks hurt so much from smiling. I was truly happy, or so I thought at the time. The smile soon turned upside down when we returned back home.

When arriving at our new home after the wedding, to my new husband's house in South Carolina, as the door got wider, the smell got stronger, and it smacked me in the face like a piece of bologna. I had to cover my nose and mouth so I wouldn't puke. I started to walk toward the kitchen, but then I stopped. Maggots everywhere, crawling over the floor, the walls, the cupboards, and even the curtains. Not something a bride wants to come home to, but I pulled up my big girl pants and got to scrubbing everything I could. Even the dishes. When I was finally done, I wanted to burn my clothes! I can see leaving some dishes on the countertop, but a consistent stream of dirty dishes set all over the house was more than I could handle. My new husband didn't have much of an explanation for this huge mess, and I felt like more of a maid than a new wife.

### Be His Own Boss

My husband had his own agenda when it came to work. He didn't like to work when the weather was warm and sunny, so my income became our main source of living. And I was not just supporting our household, but also his habits. He took advantage of this when we decided to move. We didn't have any plans on where we wanted to go, so we just drove and wound up outside of Denver, Colorado.

As we settled into our new hometown, things became more clear. I recognized the patterns that were forming in front of my eyes, and by the empty bottles I would find in my couch cushions. When I married, I was blindsided and so in love. I got comfortable with my spouse, and that's when I noticed those problems or little quirks showing their funny faces. If you love someone, you should love everything about them, including their flaws, right? That's how it started off, but eventually, I was only seeing and feeling the flaws.

The biggest flaw that I absolutely hated was when we would argue and voices would get so high that my husband would start yelling at me. I felt like I had to defend myself to someone who was acting like a boss to me, so I yelled back. I never wanted to be that person. It put me in a state of deep depression that I just wanted to end. I realized yelling was not worth me being sad and hurt. It was affecting my health.

I desperately wanted to live in peace, just feeling warm and cozy all the time. But I continued with this emotional roller-coaster ride with someone whom I couldn't trust. I just didn't understand how someone whom I loved so much would yell at me and make me feel so little. Deep down, I was starting to recognize that this was not what love was.

## Concert Ended on a Sour Note

Occasionally, like many couples, we would get together with friends and go see a concert. One particular evening at a concert, things started off well, but got heated when the alcohol was added. I tried to enjoy myself, but later that night, in the middle of the concert, my husband left our seats. And never came back. Right after the last song, I headed straight to the van where we were all supposed to meet up, hoping my husband would be, at least, around the area. He was, but he was lying on top of the van we arrived in. As soon as he saw me, he jumped down and started walking toward me. As I walked closer, I could hear him yelling, but couldn't make out the words just yet. He was saying, "Did you have funnnn?!" in a very sarcastic way. His alcohol had kicked in. The two-hour drive back felt like six, making me nervous and a little scared. By the time we got to our friend's house, my husband was ready to leave, but we all thought it would be better to stay. That night really took an emotional toll on me. I was uncertain of what to do next. Looking back now, I realize my heart emotionally left him.

Emotionally drained, the next day, I found out that my husband had been unfaithful to me in our marriage multiple times. The marriage I'd fought to keep alive was only one sided. I wondered if it was really the truth that I was hearing from the friend who told me about all of my husband's cheating, because part of me didn't want to believe it. But then I remembered back to the night my husband came home with unexplainable scratch marks that he said was a rash. I decided I physically had enough and left him.

My body, both physically and mentally, were tired of it all at that point: the cheating, lying, and being used. He wouldn't change; he was who he was. But I wanted change, so I said goodbye. As I reflect back now, most of his issues were covered well in the beginning, but it was like he kept a dusty box full of surprises for me to uncover later as our marriage progressed.

I tried way too long to make things work and hold the relationship together. Destroying myself piece by piece, staying for the wrong reasons. All the stress and chaos were affecting my health and abilities to be the woman I really was meant to be. I reached my breaking point. This was the time to really start healing and finding what love truly is for me.

Near the end of our relationship, when I had finally decided to leave, my husband confessed to all of the things that were going on behind closed doors. It didn't matter. I don't know if it was a plea for forgiveness. There is so much I can forgive, until I can't anymore. But one thing I did know was it was not too late for me to love again.

## Act 3: When I Found Myself, I Found Love

When my ex walked out of my life, we had moved back to Canandaigua, New York. I didn't know it at the time, but it was the best thing for me. I'm not saying it was easy; after living with someone for several years, I had formed a bond, a union, a friendship. But just having a friendship is not a reason to stay together. And I knew that my happiness meant something.

I'd lost what I thought was my love of a lifetime. Someone who could bring me joy, peace, and unconditional love. I discovered I didn't need someone else to feel that love. It was me all along. I used that time and the space to do a little soul searching to discover the love I had for myself. Learning to love myself from within, discovering who I was as a person, and finding what I truly wanted and desired. Sticking to my personal boundaries of joy, peace, and love and not letting anyone cross them. I took a stand and took back my physical and emotional well-being.

Being emotionally well can be a challenge. I equate it to how a dog loves you unconditionally. You're their everything, and they watch out for you. If you sneeze, their instinct is to see if you're all right. We should always be checking in on ourselves to see if we are all right. And if we discover we are not all right, we need to make it better. I had to go through a tough marriage to learn this. Knowing what love is for me was all about the deep-down connection into my soul. Finding and loving myself for who I am, not doing it for someone else or who someone thinks I should be. Building myself up, starting with self-care and boundaries, that's where true love starts.

So, much like I did after my Reiki session, I encourage you to take a deep dive into you. Even if you're not in the position I was in, take a moment to pause. Ask yourself this: am I honoring my boundaries that make me happy, or am I putting up with things that don't resonate with me? You have the power to change it up, like I did by removing myself from an unhealthy relationship. You have the power to change it up just by saying, "That doesn't feel right, so I'm going to say no." If you find yourself stuck, I'm happy to help. Let's connect!

---

RACHEL C. PATTERSON is a licensed massage therapist who carries a few healing tools on her belt. Born in the countryside of beautiful upstate New York, Rachel dreams of retiring by the water where she can walk along the sandy shore, feeling the sand between her toes and watching nightly sunsets over the water from her back porch,  living a relaxed, full life. She fills her time by crafting poetically written stories, taking pictures of nature's happenings, and snuggling with her little dog on her lap while she wire-wraps gemstones into unique jewelry pieces. She hopes one day to further her jewelry passion into silversmithing. When she gets the chance, she helps quiet women like herself open the doors to their creativity, whatever it may be. She helps them to express themselves for who they are and to ease the clutter of life. Her jewelry holds a purpose, a touchstone of calm and connection to oneself. Connect with Rachel and check out her online jewelry shop at https://bio.site/cohealingwellness.

# I Keep Myself

## Ama

"It's better than being alone" is a lie.

I was sick last week, and a friend of mine, trying to be supportive, said, "It's not like you do anything. So, unless the kids brought it home, I don't know how you could have contracted anything serious."

"It's not like you do anything. You keep to yourself."

She's right.

I do yoga and workouts in my living room. I meditate on my couch. I play in the backyard. I tell myself it's a phase, this homebound life. My youngest is *just* one, and my toddler is an incredibly challenging and wild two and a half, and I tell myself it's just a phase until they are out of these very demanding ages.

I see so many things I want to do with my kids: I want to buy them Cirque du Soleil tickets. I want to take them on a plane to see the sunset over a completely different ocean. I want to camp with them, rock climb with them, adventure with them all, but during this phase, I am paralyzed by the *how.*

How does one person wrangle four? How do I set them all up with plane snacks and entertainment? How do I get them all in seats at the circus? There is only one of me, and I am pulled in four ways, and they each need me differently. I must switch my tactic between the ages and the child, and I must consider the trends (gentle parenting) and the aesthetic (clean lines), all of which make it that much harder.

Instead, I don't do anything.
Instead, I keep to myself.

When I first met my husband, I noticed red flags from day one. But every time a fight would go a little too far or my boundaries felt discarded, I'd say to myself, *It's better than being alone*. That became a mantra, and I said it a lot more than I should have. *It's better than being alone. It's better than being alone.*

And when things really started to shift into a bad place, I would pull the mantra from the depths of my chest and say it again while on the kitchen floor or crying in the shower or shaking in the car. *It's better than being alone.*

It was a lie, actually.

Over our short marriage, I learned there's worse things than being alone or doing it all alone or not being able to take your children to the circus. There are things that can make the world incredibly dark every single morning no matter how early you rise to greet the sun and no matter how happy you *will* yourself to be.

I would have stayed in the dark, even though I scratched at my chest to try to release my heart from my own body and jumped out of the bathroom window to get away from the anger and loaded all the children in the car to get distraction-hot-chocolate just to free us from the screaming. I would have stayed there with my mantra, *It's better than being alone.*

The catalyst for leaving was simple.

The Truth.

I was able to leave when I stopped lying. I was able to leave by giving myself the gift of the truest truth, that it's better to be alone and alive than underwater and drowning.

With the truth, I am pulled in four ways all the time—just one me and four of them. With the truth, I am struggling to stretch myself across all of their needs, to keep up with which foods each likes, which extracurricular starts when. But there's no more yelling and no more scratching and no more anger. And the hot chocolate is because we just wanted it on a winter night.

There's peace. And there's quiet. And there's ... just me. Free.

These days, it's hard no matter how I do it.

It's just a phase, I tell myself as I laugh at the truth in my friend's words. You're right!

I keep to myself.

I keep myself.

I love myself, and I tell myself the truth.

---

AMA is a writer, mother, and artist. She studied contemporary dance at the University of North Carolina School of the Arts and believes dancing and writing are intertwined. She penned her first novel in the summer of '99 in a college-ruled composition book, and in the twenty-five years since, she's managed multiple online blogs, released a zine-to-mail  series called *The Glitch*, a story-to-mail series called "White," and started a small press publishing company called Aproprose Press. Her next book, *The Lightness of Being Grounded*, is slated to be available in 2025. She likes seeing her work in paper over digital and is happiest when that paper is being dog-eared and underlined. She currently lives in Charleston, South Carolina, with her four children.

# Past Where They Break

## Amanda Soesbee Kent

It's so cliché to say that in order to heal, you have to break. Worse even to endure the tired ol' "you can't have a silver lining without the cloud" adage, right? I was on a beach vacation and, to stick with the cliches, was inspired to ponder this idea while I was walking along the shore. (Two weeks at the beach with the fam is enough to break anyone, but I digress.) My youngest precious nephew had just asked his dad, my brother, to take him out in the water. "Dad! I wanna go out past where they break!" Out of the mouths of babes ...

I think that's where we all need to go sometimes, whether we want to or not. Out past where "they" break. They. The waves? Yes, but also ... the things. The things that hold us back, push us down, beat against us, keep us from moving forward. The broken trust from a friend, the abuse, the death of a loved one, the loss of a great job, the divorce, the addiction, the health scare, the mental crisis. Those are our waves, and when they break, they are monstrous.

Y'all, have you ever fought the ocean—THE WHOLE-ASS OCEAN—to get out past where the waves break? It. Hurts. And it's hard, right?! The salty water gets up your nose and in your eyes, the swirling sand scratches your sunburnt skin, the heavy surf beats your back to death as you try to shield yourself against the crash, and then you finally find your balance to stand back up and discover that you moved exactly 3.2 inches farther out.

But you *really* wanna get there, so you jump right back in again. Because it's kinda fun too! It's a challenge to get past where they break.

Wikipedia, on the all-knowing Interwebs, describes a wave break as "the critical point where linear energy turns into turbulent kinetic energy." The energy then "breaks," causing the wave to either spill, plunge, collapse, or surge. While this description is nice and clean for the physics world, it poses some real issues for those of us who, in our actual, turbulent lives, are reaching that critical point along our linear paths. We break, and then collapse or spill or plunge. What's important in the scientific description, though, is that the wave continues to move with a "distinct forward curve." Forward. Onward. Unstoppable.

I think the difference between the ocean and real life (even though one could argue that the ocean *is* life) is that in the ocean, you can physically see the point where the waves haven't started breaking yet. You can see the smooth places where you'll be able to coast, and float, and enjoy the roll of the gentler water. In life? Not so much. In real life, you can't see past where the whatever-it-is breaks. You can't see the end of the road where you'll earn that diploma or get that new job or have that baby or lose that weight or find that loving spouse or move to that new city or start that company or dump that abusive relationship or beat that cancer. In the ocean, it's easy to keep your eye on the goal and try again; but in life, instead of paddling on after you collapse and plunge underwater, you go back to shore, where it's safe. You know that place on the shore, wherever it is you started. It's comfortable on that shore, not because it's good for you, but because you know it. Will you survive there? Absolutely. The shore is ... fine.

But are *you* fine with "fine?"

I don't think I am anymore. I also wanna go out past where they break! I've stayed on the shore, not because I like it so much, but because it's familiar, and I work well in familiarity. There's a routine. It's warm on the shore, I know the people there, I can see everything around me, there are snacks ...

But this all made me start reflecting on my own journey down this rocky-ass coastline. What is "past the break" for me? What are my waves—my tsunamis—and how do I surf them? Even as I write this, I don't know if the Pandora's box of my secrets should be opened, but here goes!

I spent a very long time trying to please. Like DECADES. I needed affirmation; I needed to know that I was doing a good job, or was successful at something, or was someone's "favorite." I'm a Southern woman, a teacher, a daughter of teachers, an older sister. You know what all of those things have in common? All of them are "supposed to be ..." Supposed to be Daddy's Little Girl. Supposed to be the chosen one at school, always a teacher's pet. Supposed to be the example for my baby brother and younger cousins. Supposed to be the apron-wearing, casserole-baking, Mama's shadow pretty-pretty princess.

That's my breaking point. I have had to struggle past the fact that I am not any of those things. It sounds so silly, and the words look even more commonplace as I write them! But the desire to people-please and the lack of ability to do so has ripped me apart more than once. It's not that I wasn't able to be good at something or make the people I cared about happy. It's that I was too hung up on pleasing people in the ways they expected or wanted.

I have a distinct childhood memory of sitting at the kitchen table one evening, sobbing uncontrollably while my dad was on the phone with a softball coach he knew, trying to get me signed up for a team that season. I had purposefully let the sign-up date slip by, thinking that if we missed it, I could avoid having to play *and* having to fight with my dad. I had zero desire to play and was crushed that this was what my daddy wanted me to do. The tears weren't for softball, or Coach Paul, or my friends who played softball. The tears were for *me,* for the "me" who was not capable of making my dad proud in the manner he wanted. I hated PE class. I hated field day in elementary school. I hated the feeling of always—and, yes, I mean every single time—being picked last for whatever team sport the PE teacher was making us play that day. I hated the way I looked in gym clothes. I hated my body for not being coordinated. ("All you've gotta do is keep your eye on the ball!" Bullshit.) And that day, I hated my father for wanting me to be good at sports. I hated him for making me feel like I wasn't already good enough, and for making me believe that the only way he'd be proud was if I played that stupid sport. I wanted the things I cared about and excelled at to be enough, and right then, they weren't.

That's just one memory. Go ahead and multiply it by thirty years, and you'll have all seven salty seas full of my waves and breaks.

I recognize that I am wearing out the ocean analogies, but I don't care! In my decades of riding the currents, I have learned not to care, and that's the raft upon which I float. Dad, I love you, but if you weren't proud of me because I was never an athlete, that's a *you* problem, because I am so many other awesome things. Friend of almost twenty years, if you want to leave me out of your wedding and use the excuse that it's because you "have to ask your sorority sisters" instead of me, I can't help that. I was a "good enough" friend to earn that spot by your side, but the choice was still yours. Boyfriend, if you cheated on me after four years and a promise of marriage just because you were insecure that I had earned a college degree and you dropped out, there's nothing I can do about that. Giving up everything else for you wasn't enough; you can't have my professional success too. All along, instead of people-pleasing, I needed to learn to Amanda-please and make that my priority. Did that make me sometimes aloof, sometimes selfish, sometimes snarky. Yes. And?

So that brings us to today, to now. It's time, y'all. Get off your damn shore! Swim, paddle, dive, flail around, whatever it takes. Waves will crash and currents will pull. Tides will come and go, so be ready to go with them. But I beg you to get out past where they break, and do it sooner than I did. Yes, I would've lived a "fine" life had I stayed on that warm shore in the familiar maelstrom of trying to make myself into the person everyone wanted. But then I woke up one day and realized I wanted extraordinary, not just fine! Dive in head first—let go of fine! Your next clichéd life lesson is that Hope floats, so swim to Her.

Start right now. What are your waves? What are your breaks? Name them, speak them, know them so you'll be able to recognize them as they force the salty water up your nose and slam against your back. They won't show mercy, but they *will* roll on! Then stand up and move forward, knowing that break is past you.

# Peeling Off the Label

## Amanda Soesbee Kent

As a mature adult who knows better but does the opposite, I hypocritically label people. My favorites are the ones I call the "Coffee Shop People." Sometimes I watch the cute, trendy folks with their similar uniforms of yoga pants and giant handbags and newest-obsession water bottles and wavy blow-out hairstyles, and I eavesdrop on their conversations about soccer practice or the gym or what business trip their spouse is on, and I see the way they greet each other with one-armed hugs and *hiii-iii*s ... and a little ugly jealousy monster rears up in me and makes me wish I were one of them. Coffee Shop People, I love you so much. I love your actual labels, the curlicue monograms that you made on your Cricut and brand everything with. I love how you fit in, how you appear effortless, how the barista knows your half-baked mocha-chaka-khan order, how your SUV is always clean, how you tippity-tap on your iPhone 2001squared to update Instagram while you sit in the carpool line. I love how your house is swathed in nice neutrals, how your nails are shiny and gelled, how you have your little base of friends who are You 2.0. I see what you have, and I want it.

I always wanted a category to fit into—maybe with my trendy Coffee Shop People, or the Sorority Sisters, or the Ladies Who Lunch, or the Game Night Couples crowd. I wish people instinctively thought of me first when they had an idea to do something—"let's go out for sushi," or "let's talk about politics," or "let's start a book club," or "let's go to a Braves game." But generally, that didn't happen because I wasn't naturally a member of whatever group of people decides to do those things. Do I like to do all those things? Yep! But I'm not a group leader, and I'm not the girl who's automatically, without needing an invitation, included.

Fast forward to now. Today, at this stage in life, I proudly, yet dubiously, call myself unconventional. I slap on a Wild Card label. I don't know if it's because I secretly want a more traditional label, or because society makes me feel like we all have to fit somewhere. Either way, I have become comfortable with the idea that the category to which I belong is the one for the misfits. Do I often slip back into the "I sure wish I was a Coffee Shop Girl" mantra? Yep, and that's okay too. Being a misfit means that I recognize when not belonging is actually a form of belonging.

Y'all, I tried to be conventional—really, I did!—to the point of breaking myself and allowing my own identity to slip away. I used to be the girl who'd beg, "Can I go with you?" or hint, "I like sushi!" or offer, "I'll drive if anyone wants to go play trivia!" Just hoping. Hoping I'd get the response, "Yeah, you're in! You're one of us!" I wanted to belong, to be the one someone else envied. If I wear the same Jordache jeans everyone else has, then I'll be like them, and other people will love me too. If I pretend that I also love football, then the people who watch the games every Sunday will ask me to come. Maybe if I lost ten pounds, or could I make my hair straight? Maybe I should learn to like a certain punk band? Do I need to prance in heels at the bar instead of my boring sandals? Red lipstick or plain gloss ... what's everyone else wearing? What if I could be more Christian, or less naive, or more risky, or less academic?

I feel like it's time for some stories. I remember Nameless Classmate 1 in high school asking me if I wanted to borrow his REM cassette. (Yes, I'm "cassette tape" old.) I'd never heard of them. "Sure!" I shut myself in my bedroom and listened to the whole thing that night, numerous times, memorizing everything I could. I was gonna be one of the kids who liked that music! They were gonna be my people! Wrong. Turns out, he gave me a fake tape of some group no one had ever heard of just to see if I knew the difference. "Those kids" all got a good laugh on the bus the next day while listening to me talk about REM that wasn't actually REM.

Then Nameless Classmate 2 dared me to sneak some of my parents' whiskey to school. If I do it and don't get caught, I bet I could be part of that crowd! Wrong again. Just a dare to see if I'd be the sucker who did it. Later, Jackass Adult Boyfriend of Four Years started sleeping with the girl who cut his hair. "She's just "so real." Awesome, since I'd already ignored and pushed away my friends whom he didn't like so I could devote all my time to him.

But you know what? Maybe Haircut Girl was real. Looking back, I recognize that I sure as hell wasn't! I couldn't have defined "real" at that stage in my life if you had paid me. Though I wish I could say this was the turning point in my journey, it was more like the catalyst that sent me spiraling farther down. I was No One, to anybody. All I ever wanted was a label, something that "stuck" me to someone or something else. Mrs. Teacher Lady's Star Student. Jackass Boyfriend's Wife. Loser at School's Best Friend. The Girl Who _____. Why was that so much to ask, and why did I want it so badly? I struggled with this need for conventionality, y'all. I struggled with fitting in but also with standing out. I've always wanted to be "known," but the secret was finding out "for what."

That secret leads us here, to this very page. Do you know what my most favorite part about being in this amazing group of authors for a book collab is? Ironically, it's that I don't fit neatly into a category. I love that my writing is a wild card. I like a wild card; you never know what you're gonna get or what it's gonna be worth! Wild cards come with the anxiety of not knowing, and the fun of finding out. A label-less label, if you will indulge me with that. It has dawned on me in my late-in-life journey of discovery that I want to be known for unpredictability. I like routines and can admit that change scares me, but also ... don't plan on me upholding whatever your expectations might be. I will no longer pretend to like your likes unless I truly like them! I won't pretend that I'm a fan of your team, or that your hairstyle is one I should emulate. I don't care if my arms flap and yours don't, or that I wear my sandals in winter and you think I shouldn't, or that I'm drinking coffee at 3 p.m. and am a Southerner who hates tomatoes! This is me. If you think I should, then I probably won't.

Amanda Soesbee Kent • 31

Don't read too much piss and vinegar into this, friends. In my life now, I am quite solidly a part of an awesomely eclectic small group of people whom I love dearly. We all kind of gravitated toward each other over a few years' time, sharing some similar interests and hobbies while keeping our "other lives" as well. We are supportive of each other without question. We do the things—travel, go to festivals, have book clubs, watch the Super Bowl, talk smack about "the others." BUT even my group is unconventional; we cross a twenty-year time span in age, are at various socioeconomic stages, hold different religious viewpoints, have the oddest of family backgrounds, and can't even agree on what beers are best! It wasn't until I was moving along in my fifth decade of life that I found my people, and it happened when I stopped looking. I stopped trying to be someone else. I embraced a very lonely period of a few years when Introspection became my new best friend. I focused on me, on what I wanted, on what I needed, and on how I needed to get it. I worried less about whose feelings were getting hurt, unless they were my own. I learned to say no when I needed to, yes when I wanted to, and to be okay with my own company. I took myself to the movies; I skipped church. I had pretzels for breakfast and ice cream for supper. I slept late. I painted the downstairs bathroom pink. I didn't allow myself to feel guilty for not answering calls or returning messages. I quit acting like I needed to have extra certifications or degrees in order to be a master teacher. I stopped trying to like tomatoes! They're squishy and gross, and I have decided that I will no longer accept gross.

I want to leave you with the common image of the melancholy girl sitting at the empty bar peeling the label off of her sweating beer bottle. That's what you have to do. Sweat it out, then peel it off. Labels are unavoidable, but you can absolutely control the ones that stick. Got to go now, y'all; my friends want me to go play pickleball! This ought to be good ....

Having spent her whole life in school, AMANDA SOESBEE KENT currently teaches teenagers. Sometimes she teaches literature and writing, though usually her lessons are more about surviving life with sarcasm and wit. Amanda lives with her husband, Bill, on the family farm, where she collects rescue animals who serve no real purpose other than looking cute. Her major character  flaw is believing that everything is within a fifteen-minute time frame, whereby she allows ten minutes, hoping she can make it in seven. She has no plans to correct that flaw. However, she does plan to spend the rest of her career and life soaking up as many new books and producing as many new writings as she can, for her greatest love is words.

# A Junkyard Dog's Secret to Saving the World:

## A Primer on Boundaries and Trust

### Cindy Urbanski

After living "who knows where" for two years, Bugsy, the junkyard dog, came to us from a kill shelter run by animal control. He was fifteen pounds underweight, heartworm positive with a rocking case of kennel cough, and on high alert at all times. He also smiled at us, wagged his tail in a circle, and tried to fit into our laps.

Now, four months later, Bugsy can freely sleep on his back on the comfy bed, instead of the "safety" of the cage. He zooms, with abundant joy and reckless abandon, around the backyard and then rolls in the fresh grass to point his belly toward the sun. He feels well and secure enough to be his amazing dog self. Isn't that what we are all seeking? Isn't that what we all deserve? Don't we crave in our deepest souls the freedom to be vulnerable in a world that seems so very broken and scary?

Watching Bugsy let his guard down and trust us reminded me of something I've learned many times over as a human. Such freedom doesn't come simply with big love like we have for Bugsy. It comes with boundaries. Set firmly and compassionately. And, because we are grown people, not dogs, we set those boundaries for ourselves, and we hold them. And that is what allows us the comfort to turn our soft spots toward the sun and offer healing to the world.

In our dog's case, we had so much love to offer. We took him home, gave him a name (Bugsy Calhoun because we busted him outta the joint), and got him started on heartworm and kennel cough treatment. My husband hustled off to the grocery store, so my son and I made twenty-two quarts of what we call "Granny's Magic Dog Food." It's a recipe my mother created for her beloved old dog that prolonged his life for many, many years. It is truly magical. I'll include it here at the end.

We also set firm boundaries by immediately starting Bugsy's training. No barking at the windows or the fence. No throwing himself against the front door at the sound of the UPS person. Leash training. Place training. A gentle mouth with cheese snacks (allll the medicine hidden within). Waiting to be released before eating. All the things that make for a good dog, and more importantly, a happy one.

You see, a dog with manners is a happy dog because he knows he does not have to be in charge of every single thing. His people have it! We will let him know if there is a problem that he needs to deal with; otherwise, he can relax and, well, be a dog. No need for high alert. These boundaries were our gift to him.

And, for the first month, Bugsy had a hard time settling. Oh, he would sit and stay on his place because we told him to, but if released, he would trot around the house, looking for threats or something to eat, at first himself and then all of us. He actually preferred to sleep in a crate rather than on a soft bed because he felt safer there. He liked the *idea* of the dog bed at the foot of ours, but once the lights went out and it got quiet, he would take himself to the hard, cold floor of the crate.

I'll never forget the first night I heard him settle into the dog bed and heave a huge, satisfied sigh. He didn't make it through the whole night without heading to the cage, but he was there for much longer.

As the days went by, he showed us his belly, trotted around the house less, and sighed more, and his sighs relaxed everyone in the house, because all relaxed dogs are service dogs; they lower human heart rates and quell anxiety.

Now, when he sees someone passing the house or a package delivered, he comes to find me and tell me. He doesn't bark; he simply talks.

He loves to nap on the porch at my feet while I write. He *can* run through the dog door anytime, into the back yard. He can see all the way up the street and note the passersby. Yet he's sound asleep, trusting me to watch and let him know if his services will be needed.

On our walks, he carries his eighty pounds of healthy muscle right at my side and ignores everything, even the cats we find along the way. Unless he doesn't. He's a work in progress, just like all of us.

I think the secret here is in the trust building. Bugsy the junkyard dog is finally comfortable because he trusts us. He trusts us to feed him. He trusts us to know whether or not there is danger that he needs to attend. He trusts he is home.

BIG love *is* boundary setting to some degree. Boundaries breed trust, and trust breeds a home. And, as I said at the onset, we are grown adults, not dogs, so we get to set these boundaries firmly for ourselves. And when we set the boundaries that make us feel safe and hold the line on those boundaries, we can trust ourselves and relax; we can trust ourselves to know what other humans we can trust. And in that trust in ourselves, and through that trust in others whom we deem worthy, we find a home, and we are free.

It took me decades to learn this particular secret. I didn't trust anyone because I didn't trust myself. I didn't trust myself because I allowed people to blow through any boundaries I happened to set. I didn't feel safe in my own trustworthiness, and without boundaries, like Bugsy, I was on high alert, ready to protect and defend those closest to me at all times. I was trapped. I could *never* be vulnerable and show my soft spots.

So here's the secret: boundaries *are* compassion. I find that boundaries are not only an act of loving on myself, but also the ultimate act of loving on my people and showing compassion to the world. Post learning the secret of a good boundary, I can be found rolling in the grass on occasion, soft spots on display, in the home I have created with those I have trusted myself to trust. I can even show those soft spots to the world when I so choose, because I know my trusted ones have me. And my people are in that grass right beside me and out in the world because they know *I* have *them*. My heart explodes with joy as we all roll along together, and in this explosion, we all are able to spread our huge compassion out into a world that so desperately needs it.

## Granny's Magic Dog Food

Please note this recipe is for educational purposes only. Consult your veterinarian before changing anything related to your pet's diet. Recipe makes 22 quarts.

### Ingredients

- 1 cup rolled oats
- 2 cups brown rice
- 1 pound lentils
- 1 pound pinto beans or black-eyed peas
- 3 pounds kale
- 3 pounds sweet potatoes
- 2 pounds carrots
- 1 head cauliflower
- 2 crowns broccoli
- 1 bunch celery
- 1 dozen eggs
- 1 pound chicken gizzards
- 1 pound liver
- 6 pounds chicken, bone in and skin on (We use thighs.)
- 6 pounds pork, fattiest cut you can find (We use a Boston butt.)

### Instructions

#### Night Before

1. Soak lentils and pinto beans in water.
2. Cook pork butt in Crock-Pot on low overnight.

#### Day of ... Chicken First

1. Cook chicken in your biggest pot with just enough water to cover.
2. Remove chicken and set aside to cool.

#### Veggies Next

1. Bake sweet potatoes first.
2. Chop carrots, cauliflower, broccoli, and celery.
3. Add oats and rice to beans.

4. Add chopped veggies to broth from chicken and add enough water to cover. (If your pot isn't big enough, use two.)
5. Cook veggies until really tender.
6. Add kale at the end. Break it off of the stalk and rip it into chunks. Stir it in a little at a time. It wilts.
7. Fill 1-quart containers half full with veggie/grain mix and let cool.
8. Add sweet potatoes WITH peel.
9. Scramble eggs and add to veggie-filled containers evenly.

## Meat Last

1. Cook gizzards and livers in a pot.
2. Debone and cut chicken into bite-sized chunks. Include skin.
3. Shred pork.
4. Add meat to cooled veggies evenly.

## Gourmet Level

1. Add a bit of fresh rosemary or parsley (or BOTH!) when serving. It's good for digestion.
2. Add a scoop of yogurt on top when serving, for gut health.

---

CINDY URBANSKI is a mom of three for now. (She solidly counts her son-in-law as one of her children and hopes to add more to the brood someday when her son finds his person.) She loves cooking wholesome food, reading good books, traveling and being in the woods or near the water with her husband, her children, and her dog. She is also the  lead writing coach for Synergy Publishing Group and a yoga instructor, both occupations that tap into her super power of helping people love on themselves. Cindy is fearlessly accepting, wildly authentic, persistently truthful, and relentlessly kind. Connect with her on Instagram: @cindy_d_urbanski and check out her website at cindyurbanski.com.

# How to Be an Artist:
## Seven Lessons from an Art Life

---

### Fran Gardner

---

My first oil painting lesson with my grandmother happened when I was about seven years old. Not in a studio, she had no studio, but in her kitchen. It was a painting of a magnolia blossom on a red velvet drape. I worked at it, hard, because I was discovering shape, value, color; I was learning to see. But mostly, I worked at it because I was getting validation from a woman whom I respected, who put her full attention on me, who saw something in me while I struggled to paint an awkward still life. She handed me a dream that day. To be an artist is to see the lessons in nearly everything, then adding those lessons to the lens of our creative lives.

How to Be an Artist #1
## Honor the guides who are placed in your path.

We didn't start with crayons or chalk; we started with oil paints, the real thing. A burnished wooden box with old and disused paints, the silver tubes mashed and cracked, their labels sticky with leaking oil, the bottle of linseed yellowed but still liquid, usable. Brushes with patinaed handles, but clean and pliable bristles. It was a treasure, better than costume jewelry, better than the silver tea service, better than the unused upstairs rooms of that old house, piled with *Life* magazines and cardboard boxes filled with the debris of life and family. Her name was Elizabeth; I called her Dossie;

she was my first art teacher. She raised five boys—my father and four uncles. By the time I came along, I think she was just so grateful to finally have a girl child. I imagine she put her paint box away when she got married, tried not to think about it, and started having children. But, years later, she saw something in me, and she thought of that box; she might ought to point the way, and we weren't pretending. We would start with nothing less than real art materials. My first guide, this wise grandmother, trusted me with her gift. Over time, I realized that she gave me much more than a box of old paints. She gave me the art life that she could not have. I accepted it.

How to Be an Artist #2
## Difficulty is a reason to confront and explore.

I don't think I ever uttered the professor's first or last name when speaking with her. She was absolutely terrifying. More direct than anyone I had ever met, uncensored, bursting with her thoughts and opinions, argumentative. And also erudite, eloquent, expressive. A brilliant lecturer. During class one day, her New York, or maybe Brooklyn, accent—clipped, quick, staccato—clashed with my Southern accent—languid, melodic, drawn. It was clear she made an assumption about me based not on the question I asked at the end of the lecture, but the sound of my voice, my region of the country. I had a decision to make. Ignore her embarrassing call-out about my accent or confront her. After the lecture, I waited until the room cleared. She was bracing for a confrontation. I invited her to lunch. She reacted with surprise, curiosity, pleasure—I had stepped up to her challenge. Over cafeteria food, I told her I wanted to learn how to analyze a work of art like she did. She told me she was sorry for her hurtful behavior, her misjudgment. By the end of lunch, she was my faculty mentor. Bravery takes us into our deepest fears and our most tender spaces. It isn't easy. But often, beyond the apprehension is a deep and lasting reward.

How to Be an Artist #3
## Allow it to speak, and trust that it is saying something relevant.

Prepare for eight weeks of physical therapy. Prepare for difficult navigation. Prepare for re-learning how to go up and down stairs. Prepare for pain. I was prepared. And then I wasn't. I managed the pain; I learned how to do the stairs; I figured out how to move around the house; I went to far more than eight weeks of physical therapy. But the most taxing, the most challenging was the almost imperceptible rate of healing. I expected a slow but steady climb; imagine a line trending upward. What I got was plateaus, a sudden, slight, but noticeable improvement, then nothing for a while, a very long while. My heart, the empathic believer, told me to trust that the body would do its job refiring nerve endings, regrowing traumatized tissue. But my head, that pesky data gatherer, constantly reminded me that I was not experiencing any discernible change, sometimes for weeks, nagging me that something was wrong. Then suddenly, a little more range of motion, a little less pain, another plateau at that level, building anticipation toward the next micro shift in improvement, brain and heart in battle over whether to doubt or to trust. In my art, I often include sewing, both machine and hand stitching. These passages, textural and colorful, are also time consuming and tedious. Having the patience to make art that is hand sewn tricked me into believing it is only about enduring. But my other teacher, knee surgery, taught me that it is also, and sometimes more importantly, about allowing and trusting.

How to Be an Artist #4
## Have the tenacity to stay with it until it teaches you something.

I started taking Brent meals during COVID, when we broke our quarantine once a week to sit on his back porch, masked and socially distanced. He was a consummate archivist, my colleague and friend. He loved wine, but his drug of choice was laughter, the wine bringing us there quicker, no time to waste. He had ALS, or amyotrophic lateral sclerosis, a progressive neurodegenerative disease that affects nerve cells in the brain and spinal cord, otherwise known as Lou Gehrig's disease. In those uncertain and frightening days of COVID, stretching to weeks and months, our weekly visits became a sort of therapy for both of us. He bragged to friends about how I brought him delicacies—venison burgers, wild hog sausages, quail, and pheasant. My hunter husband means this is the food we regularly eat, fresh and locally sourced. Healthy, clean food I reasoned, for Brent and for us. I made a vow, not to Brent but to myself, that I would continue those weekly visits, complete with a meal, for as long as he could eat and beyond that to whatever happened next. Our time together changed when his condition worsened. First, he asked me to administer his infusions. My response was, "But I'm an artist," and we both laughed through it. Then he needed my help going to the bathroom. My response was, "But I'm an artist," and we both laughed through it. Each deepening and frightening level of his worsening condition brought the same—his confidence and trust in me to do the difficult thing that he was brave enough to ask me for, and my fear of doing something wrong and hurting him, my fear that as an artist, I was not up to this challenge. My art has taught me to stay with a piece, even when it is frustrating, even when it is a mess, even when, even when. So I stayed in our friendship, even when, even when. Brent taught me that there is humility in asking for help, that we can ask for the easy things, like venison burgers, or the hard things, like holding a dying person's hand. He taught me that it is possible to accept the thing that is impossible to accept. He taught me that there is grace in dying. He taught me to laugh through it. I'm still trying.

How to Be an Artist #5
## Be brave enough to revise.

An often asked question of an artist is "how do you know when it is finished?" Every artist answers this question differently because it is a different answer for every artist. As we become skillful in our management of materials, our compositional awareness, and our unique messages, we develop a sense of where to end. I don't let work out of my studio until it is satisfying for me. But occasionally, one slips through. Once, I tore up a piece that had been in a New York exhibit. I had my photograph taken with it in the gallery. Brought my daughter, her boyfriend, and my nephew to the opening. Isn't that one of the hallmarks of success? Wasn't this proof of accomplishment? When I saw it on exhibit, on that clean, white gallery wall in New York, it just wasn't true. It had the right elements, but the structure was all wrong. Thankfully, it didn't sell, because as soon as it was shipped back to my South Carolina studio, I took it out of the box and deconstructed it. This is when the reworking began, studying the piece with my critical self, working back into it with my creative self. Back and forth until the revised thing emerged, related to the earlier piece, but significantly changed. Into a museum show it went, reworked, reassembled, revised—a new version of itself, stronger and more resonant. I don't determine the amount of time it takes to make a piece, nor do I really care. I like the studio; I want to be there. I want to spend vast amounts of time with my art, with each piece. I want to learn from it, to lean into that gut feeling, that little tug, that whisper that says, "It doesn't matter how much studio time it is taking, who likes it, or where it has been; if I'm not comfortable, if it doesn't fit, it isn't right." Revision is an ongoing process. We are constantly working and reworking, doing and redoing, modeling and remodeling, constructing and reconstructing. I fix it, then I fix it again, and maybe again. Each version richer and deeper.

How to Be an Artist #6
## Explore your full sensory range.

Artists, like other disciplines—doctors, engineers, historians, etc.— come together for networking and sharing of ideas. They call theirs conferences or symposia; we call ours retreats. Many years ago, Beau, an accomplished artist and dear friend (whom I met at a retreat) said, "Let's do our own retreat." It was like when we were kids and someone said, "Let's do a play," and so we did. Producer and director, she has organized, and I have led artist retreats ever since. In every retreat, at least one artist's eyes will well up with tears, and since I'm a sympathetic crier, mine will too. The artist will immediately apologize for this emotional display, as we are taught to do. Our tears are just not acceptable in our culture. But the retreat is not "our culture." It is a cloistered community of caring, support, sharing, trust. It is the very place where tears should and can be shed. I emphasize this to my retreat artists: We have five senses—sight, smell, touch, taste, and hearing. These are just the obvious ones. In reality, we experience in other ways. Spatial awareness, empathy, intuition—

these also help us tune into the world to understand when we are in danger, or in love, or in protective mode, or in a safe environment. The art we make comes from that deep sensory place. It is the work of our souls. We should be touching those most vulnerable places when we do this work. And when we speak of it, sometimes tears come before we can find words. The more I commit to this path, this giving in to all of the sensory information, the more I find rhythm in the work, the deeper the work grows and becomes thoroughly satisfying and layered with message and meaning. I hope doctors, engineers, and historians are also doing this.

How to Be an Artist #7
## Recognize your teachers.

Those good pieces, the bulk of our work, are where we hone the relationship to our materials, where we practice shifts in compositional arrangements, where we learn how these materials and compositions combined create our unique voices. This is the pathway of how our good work becomes better over time. But what about those great pieces? The ones that are so surprising it almost feels like we are channels for a divine message? I've had a few of those pieces; you probably have too. Years ago, I made an entire series of twenty-one pieces over the course of two years and had no idea where these poignant, sometimes painful and sometimes joyful, images were coming from. I titled the series Arcana, suggesting the secret knowledge that I suspected these pieces held, but didn't really understand. Looking back on it, the series foretold a painful divorce, a pathway to healing, and a surprising and treasured future. These are moments when our work, whatever it is, surprises us, makes us feel like it is coming through us, not from us. These are our teachers, our prophets, our guides. This is the work that is pointing the direction, urging you to pay attention. I have had several such teachers, works of art that I can't tell you how I made them because they came through me, not from me. A very wise teacher, Lee, a mentor and friend, told me to keep these pieces close and look at them often. A bit of good advice that I followed and am thankful for. I kept most of these pieces;

they are in my home. I look at them every day. They are my beacons, wayfinders guiding me toward my most illuminating and inspiring work.

We are all creative beings making up our lives as we go along, every day anew, accumulating lessons. The lessons are teachers challenging us even when we stubbornly resist. The lessons are situations that cause us to walk unexpected and difficult paths with switchbacks and blind curves. The lessons are betrayal and disappointment, aging bodies and unforeseen illnesses. They come from friends and enemies. They come from joy and delight. They come from trial and error, sometimes lots of errors. Each on its own impactful, but amassed, they create the multifaceted lenses through which we understand and process our world. These lessons—our collective body of knowledge, the layers of our oil paintings, the patchwork of our quilts.

---

FRAN GARDNER is distinguished professor emerita of art and art history at the University of South Carolina Lancaster where she taught studio courses and art history for thirty-two years. Through these many years of teaching, she developed her methods for working with artists on their studio practice and creativity and gained the expertise for writing about art, leading retreats, teaching workshops, and judging and curating exhibitions. She works in mixed media collage with a heavy emphasis on fiber arts. She paints and draws with traditional materials, but also with thread, layering her work with rich texture, color, and mark-making. She is the author of *Artists Will Find a Way: A Studio Navigation Guide*. Learn more about Fran's work at frangardnerart.com.

# Am I Losing My Mind?

## Jennifer Howe

### Prelude

This one's for you, Mom.

I looked down the other day and saw my mother's hands. They were a bit chapped from the cold weather, a few of the finger nails had jagged edges, and there were some new wrinkles.

But none of that truly mattered. Her hands held memories that her brain could no longer hold.

Her hands rocked me as an infant, helped me cross the street on my first day of kindergarten, tied my shoes over and over again, and rubbed my back when I couldn't sleep.

Her hands clapped the loudest at my dance recital, wrote funny notes on my lunch napkins, and squeezed me tight during the Lord's Prayer in church.

Her hands baked chocolate chip cookies, braided my hair, and pulled the seat belt tighter when I was learning to drive.

Her hands wiped tears from her eyes the first time she caught a glimpse of me in my wedding dress, showed me how to bathe my babies, and picked up the phone to find out what was happening in North Carolina when I moved eight hundred miles away.

Her imperfect hands have left a perfectly loving impression on me. These are my mother's hands.

I looked down the other day and saw my mother's hands. The funny yet scary thing was that my mother's hands were attached to my arms.

## I

I opened the pantry door, turned on the light, and paused. What did I need to get in here? I couldn't remember. My heart started beating fast. I felt beads of sweat forming on my brow. Was I looking for a drink? A quick after work snack? No. Not thirsty or hungry.

Don't panic. Think. Think harder. Right, I need to grab the can of diced tomatoes to finish cooking dinner, a taco rice dish I saved from Facebook. Can in hand, I turned off the light and shut the door. I took a deep breath. My heart slowed down. I could smell the hamburger mixed with taco seasoning simmering on the stove.

Why did I panic? That is the million dollar question. I have a lot on my mind. Between work, my husband, two teenagers, two dogs, soccer practices, and baseball games, there is a lot going on. I can forget about a can of $0.89 diced tomatoes from Harris Teeter once in a while, right? I mean, that should be allowed.

At least I know where my car keys are.

I know what day of the week it is.

I know who the president of the United States is.

When my son, Tyler, had a suspected concussion after clashing with another player on the high school soccer field last season, the trainer asked him, "What day is it?" and "Who is the president?" He answered with Wednesday and Joe Biden. The trainer said he was okay. I must be okay too.

I'll admit my secret. The one that sometimes keeps me up at night. The secret that has me playing rounds of solitaire and word searches on my iPad in an effort to keep my mind sharp and engaged.

I am afraid of getting Alzheimer's.

There, I have finally said it.

When I forget something, I automatically think, "Could I have early onset Alzheimer's?" An irrational reaction? I am really not sure.

Alzheimer's has affected my family in indescribable ways. My grandmother, my mother, and my aunt all passed from Alzheimer's. In an eight-year stretch of time, I lost three of the most important women in my life. A coincidence? I don't know for sure, but I don't think so.

## II

My mom was diagnosed with early onset Alzheimer's when she was fifty-eight years old. I am fifty.

According to the National Institute on Aging, when the disease develops before the age of sixty-five, it's considered early onset. And according to researchers at the Mayo Clinic, on average, people with Alzheimer's disease live between three and eleven years after diagnosis. My mom passed eight years after her diagnosis at the age of sixty-six.

So getting Alzheimer's scares me more than the two diagnoses I already have, diabetes and chronic kidney disease.

I was diagnosed with type 2 diabetes five years ago. After months of feeling "not quite right" and not knowing why, I had an answer. It wasn't a complete surprise as it runs in my family; my dad is diabetic. I also had gestational diabetes during both of my pregnancies. While diabetes isn't always easy, it is something I can manage and doesn't interrupt my day-to-day living. I routinely check my blood sugars, take my medicine, and watch what I eat (for the most part).

In 2022, after a routine physical, it was discovered, through blood work, that my kidney function was compromised. The nephrologist diagnosed me with chronic kidney disease, stage three. He told me I had the kidney of an eighty-five-year-old woman. I was forty-eight. He also said I could live a long, healthy life, as long as I stay in stage three. So far, so good. But we needed to find the cause, which unfortunately still remains unknown.

The nephrologist ruled out diabetes as the cause, as there were no high levels of protein in my urine. I was referred to a rheumatologist for autoimmune tests, which came back clear, and a kidney biopsy didn't reveal a cause either. They asked if I'd had COVID-19 or another viral infection. The truth is, not to my knowledge.

I am a mystery. A mystery whose kidney function is staying stable.

I like to think of myself as a glass half full type of person, at least most of the time. I have a way of seeing the good in a situation. But when I think too much about Alzheimer's and the courageous battle my mom fought with the unrelenting disease, the glass can teeter between being half full and half empty.

What a crazy disease. It may leave your body healthy, but takes your mind and memories away.

That is what I am afraid of. If I don't have my memories, what do I have? I am not afraid of forgetting that I had peanut butter toast with bananas for breakfast or that I dislike thunderstorms and tornado warnings. I am afraid I will forget what it felt like trying on wedding dresses and finding "the one" or the unconditional love I felt meeting my babies for the first time. Worse, what if I forget I am Tyler and Molly's mom or Todd's wife?

That is what happened to my mom. She was healthy enough, but could not remember what she ate for breakfast or to turn the coffee pot off. As the disease progressed, things got worse, and there were moments when she did not know where she was or who her immediate family was.

However, as her journey with Alzheimer's continued, she remained a woman of faith. A devout Catholic, her motto in life was, "Do your best. God will do the rest."

With a joyful heart, endless patience, a smile that lit up the room, and an infectious laugh, she let God work through her to bring comfort to those around her as she battled Alzheimer's, even toward the end of her disease.

Believe it or not, there are some very good moments and days with such an exasperating disease. We celebrated those days. To be quite honest, those times taught me more about my mom.

### III

Nine months after Todd and I were married, we moved from Massachusetts to North Carolina for a job opportunity. We were the first ones to "leave home." We didn't have children yet, which made it just a bit easier. Nineteen years later, I can say it was the right move for us, but it did leave us eight hundred miles away or a twelve-hour drive from family and friends.

My parents came to visit us in Huntersville, North Carolina, in May one year, right around my mom's birthday and Mother's Day. She tolerated the drive okay and wasn't too confused to be out of her familiar surroundings. I will admit that buying presents for her was getting harder, so I wanted to get her something she needed. I picked out a pair of simple blue tennis shoes from Target. The ones they hang on the rack, no box needed. This was what Dad had said she needed. When she tried them on, they didn't fit. No problem. I would return them while they were visiting. She wanted to come with me to pick out some new ones. Okay. My dad came too.

We got to Target and guided her to the shoe department. I had her sit on the bench, and I brought her some tennis shoes to try on. She looked at me with a bright smile and asked, "How did you know to buy me these shoes?" I think I gave her a confused look. She then said, "When I was growing up, my aunt and uncle always bought me a new pair of tennis shoes for my birthday. I always looked forward to opening their gift and trying on my new shoes. I miss them so much, and now you have bought me new shoes." I never knew this but was so glad I could make her happy. I was fascinated that she could remember back all those years but couldn't remember what store we were in or what we had eaten for lunch an hour ago.

My mom wasn't an avid reader. She preferred looking through magazines to picking up a two-hundred-plus page book. But she never missed an opportunity to read to a child, whether it was her own children (there are four of us), her students, or her five grandchildren.

My son, Tyler, came home from daycare one evening and asked me to sing the great big spider song. I said, "Do you mean the itsy bitsy spider song?" He replied, "No, I really mean the great big spider song. If you don't know it, can you please call Memere? She will know it because she is a teacher." Okay. Here goes nothing. I picked up the phone, called my mom, and explained the situation.

Although she had accepted that she could no longer drive at this point, she was still working as a transitional kindergarten teacher at a Catholic school in Western Massachusetts.

"Put Tyler on the phone please," she said. I hit the speaker button, as I wasn't going to miss this. In a big, deep, gravelly voice, my sweet mom started singing about the great big spider to the tune of, you guessed it,

"The Itsy Bitsy Spider." Tyler's whole face lit up. "That's it. She knows it! I knew she would know it." At that moment, she was both of our heroes. Alzheimer's be damned. Later that year, my mom bought Tyler a copy of the itsy bitsy spider book for Christmas. It still sits on his bookshelf today, and he just finished his junior year of high school.

Molly was three when she asked my mom to read her a story. My mom happily agreed, and Molly ran off to get a book, then settled herself on the couch next to Memere. I was a little nervous. Alzheimer's is unpredictable, to say the least. What if my mom forgot a word? What if Molly corrected her, as only my spirited three-year-old could (it is Molly)? What if this wasn't a good idea? I watched them together, heads bent over the book. I even snuck a picture. I had nothing to worry about; they both made it flawlessly through the book. This was a good day with the disease; they both did great. To this day, that picture remains a favorite.

I was with my mom the Christmas before she passed (in February, two short months later). There was no doubt that her Alzheimer's was progressing at a fast rate. I had a feeling I needed to cherish this time with her, and I was right. My immediate and extended family had gathered at my cousin's house. I was sitting with my mom, and she asked me to get her husband. She was ready to go home. She told me it was a nice party, but that she didn't know anybody. I told her that everyone was family. She didn't believe me, as she didn't see her mom or dad. She didn't realize that they had passed. Her mind was reverting back to when she was in her early twenties.

She was quite surprised to learn that the woman sitting on the couch five feet away was her sister and best friend. She was even more surprised to learn that she had four children. She looked at me, and said, "Who are my children?" I looked back at her and said, "I am one of your daughters." With a great big smile and love in her eyes, she said, "You are? Well this is great because you are so nice."

Instead of feeling sad, I realized she had just given me a gift. I got to experience the raw emotion a mother feels the first time she sees her child. I had never felt so loved as I did at that moment.

# Postlude

My mom taught me so much in the forty-three years we had together. Some practical things and some things that may seem strange to others, but comfort me, even now. Most importantly, she taught me how to be a mom.

I hated having my hair washed as a child. I would scream so loudly that the neighbors would come over to see what was happening. My mom would say, "We are just washing Jenny's hair." I think I was afraid of getting soap in my eyes. The solution? My mom would tell me to lift my head up, close my eyes, and pretend to watch my favorite cartoon on the ceiling. At that time, I loved the *Flintstones*. "What do you see, Jenny? What is Fred doing now?" It worked like a charm. I calmed down, and I have had clean hair ever since.

She packed our lunches every day. On special occasions, she would sneak a little note in with our desserts and even wrapped our sandwiches on our birthdays. One Halloween, I found two small wrapped presents in my lunch box with a note that said "trick or treat?" One package was a block, obviously the trick, and the other was a small piece of candy, the treat. While it may have been a little over the top, I loved it. The little things. I have done similar things for my kids.

My siblings and I hated taking medicine when we were little. I still hate taking my meds, but I do it. We insisted it wouldn't taste good. And her response, "This is really laughing medicine. As soon as you swallow it, you will start laughing. You will be laughing so hard that you won't even taste it." Once again, she was right. How could you not laugh when you swallowed it? Can't get my kids to buy into this one, but they laugh knowing I bought into it.

Family bowling was a thing we did, but back in the '70s and '80s, there weren't gutter guards. Kids today have it so much easier. I mean, today, they also don't walk uphill both ways to school. But I digress. Whenever one of our bowling balls was headed toward the gutter, my mom would have us all lean in the opposite direction, willing the ball to switch course. It worked every once in a while and made me laugh every time. I still lean in the opposite direction of my bowling ball.

I liked snacks. I still do. When we would ask for an afternoon snack, my mom would ask us some important questions. "Where is your lunch at? Is it between your belly and knees, or is it at your toes?" If you answered between your belly and knees, you could have a snack. If you answered at your toes, no snack. Time to make supper.

My mom did not use bad words a lot, but there was an occasional "oh sh-t." The words she hated the most were "shut up." That one was never allowed in our house, no matter how old you were. Once, we asked her how old we needed to be to say "sh-t." Without skipping a beat, she said, "When you are thirteen, you can say sh-t." That sounded amazing at eleven years old. On my thirteenth birthday, I received a house key and permission to say "sh-t!" It was a right of passage. Strange but true! And it has become a right of passage for my nieces, cousin's kids, and my own two kids.

She was low-key when it came to makeup and beauty products. Less was more. But the one thing she always had on hand was a tube of lipstick. She would put some on her lips and then rub a little bit on her checks for a dash of color. Then there was her Jean Nate. She didn't leave home without a little splash. To her, it was a clean and refreshing scent. How can you argue with that? While I don't put lipstick on my checks, I am in the habit of using a little blush on my checks, and I have been known to spray a little Bath and Body Works Gingham scent on before leaving the house.

Watching your mom struggle with memory loss is hard. Thinking that you might struggle with it at some point is hard too. But for today, I am grateful to be making memories with my family and remembering the memories I made with my mom.

JENNIFER HOWE is a writer who gains inspiration from her hectic, never dull life as a wife, mom, and full-time communications professional. She and her husband, Todd, live in Huntersville, North Carolina, with their two teenagers, Tyler and Molly. If Jennifer isn't home, you can find her at the field watching Tyler play baseball, on the sidelines of the pitch cheering on Tyler and Molly in their soccer matches, or in the bleachers watching Molly on the basketball court. In her spare time, which is a little over forty hours a week, Jennifer has the privilege of serving as director of campus and community communications at the University of North Carolina Charlotte. You can follow her @jennifer.arsenaulthowe on Facebook.

# Other People

## Tonya Reid

"You have cancer!" someone says clear as day in my ear. I am jolted from my slumber. I sit upright in bed and immediately look around the room. I rip the covers off, fumbling with my tangled nightshirt to try and give myself a half-assed breast exam. Shaking the fog from my brain, I am freaking out in a hotel room in the most magical place on earth, Disney World.

I slowly start to remember where I am and what's going on. Okay. That's right. I'm at Pop Century Hotel. My husband, Billy Reid, is in the shower. We had to set the alarm for the ass crack of dawn to use some app to grab a reservation for the park's newest ride. He told me I didn't have to get up yet, so I went back to sleep.

But not sleep, sleep. More like some twilight zone, in-between sleep. The kind of sleep where you know you're getting to sleep. The delicious space between the hell's bells I gotta get up and the REM cycle. Delicious unless someone abruptly whispers in your ear, "You have cancer!"

We surprised our son, Chris, and his family the day before by showing up at the gift shop in the hotel lobby. Our grandkids were looking to blow the spending money we had given them since we had convinced them that we were not going to be joining them, all the while knowing our reservations were intact at the same hotel. Our four boys grew up going to Disney like some kids get to go to the mall or the movies. They can thank their ADHD, big kid, ride-loving father for that. Billy Reid would be devastated as each one of them, one by one, reached a certain age that friends or school or job obligations kept them from wanting to or being able to go. I became his sole Season Pass Holder pal until the boys began having kids or until they became nostalgic for their youth and started coming back around.

Translation: Pops is footing or supplementing the bill?! I didn't just win the Super Bowl, but vacations are expensive, adulting isn't as much fun as I thought it would be, *and* I'm going to Disney World, with my dad!

I, myself, was thick in the throes of the delightful season of my life called menopause. About six months earlier while standing behind the chair at my salon, foiling what felt like client number four hundred and fifty-two of the day, with sweat rolling down parts of my body I didn't realize I had, and pleading out loud for anyone on my team passing by to PLEASE BRING ME MY PEARLS ... my pearls being a freezable necklace called Hot Girl Pearls that I kept in the fridge for what was becoming a multiple times a day occurrence of near self-combustion. A client suggested I consider going to talk to her hormone replacement doctor. Which I did. And I was a few months into a bioidentical hormone replacement regimen.

Right then and there, I decided I shouldn't be messing with Mother Nature's chemistry set and stopped cold-turkey taking the estrogen, progesterone, testosterone cocktail that had been prescribed for me. Back home, a checkup with my doctor alleviated some concern. However, I couldn't seem to shake the weird, all-too-real experience I'd had on vacation.

Months rolled by, and Chris came home for Thanksgiving with his wife, Tiffany, and their two kids, Lucy and Max. The entire weekend he complained about a pinched nerve in his neck. He'd been to the chiropractor on the way out of town, and they'd only provided temporary relief. He would incessantly insist that every time he reached to pick up his drink with his left hand, his arm would give out. Being the nurturing mother of boys, I told him to pick up his damn drink with his other hand and quit whining. He kept saying that he felt off.

Back home in Mount Pleasant, South Carolina. Chris went to see his chiropractor again. Thank Gawd, the chiropractor wasn't dismissive like I had been. It's so easy to be that way with the people we are the closest to. Especially if they tend to update you regularly with everything that is bugging them, be it physical ailments or life in general. They start to sound like Charlie Brown's teacher, "Wah, wah. Wah, wah, wah, wah." The doctor sent him to MUSC, The Medical University of South Carolina, in downtown Charleston to rule out a stroke since his symptoms sounded as such and to have an MRI to see what was actually going on.

At 9:00 p.m. on Monday, November 29, 2021, our lives were changed forever. Our thirty-nine-year-old son was diagnosed with a brain tumor. A stage 4 glioblastoma brain tumor. Excuse me? Can you repeat that? WHAT? A brain tumor? He was the healthiest looking one in the family. The one who worked out all of the time. The one who didn't need to lose weight. The athletic one. This is what happens to *other people*.

Until *you* are the other people. Or someone you love becomes *the other people*.

It's odd how the Universe works. In the spring of 2021, we sold the building that housed our salon, and I joined my husband in retirement. Filled with the excitement of being empty nesters, both personally and professionally, we'd begun making our future wish lists, which included new travel destinations, new experiences, new skills honed for our second act. Little did I realize that my path was being cleared to be available and fully present to the needs of our family.

Our travel destinations looked more like the oncology waiting rooms at MUSC and Duke University Medical Center than poolside cabanas. The mountains we climbed were of the emotional, gut-wrenching variety versus the scenic ones. The trails we traversed were the shortest routes from the clinical trials where Chris received the latest round of radiation or chemo to the parking decks we were becoming all too familiar with. Instead of joining an improv troupe or mastering mah-jongg, new skills honed were along the lines of knowing which pharmacies were most likely to have medications on hand to fill prescriptions in a timely manner, managing doctor appointments while making surprise lunchtime appearances with coveted culinary contraband to show Lucy and Max some love, or learning to anticipate and avoid what might trigger anxiety at any moment for anyone involved.

Overnight, our second act took the shape of first responders.

Fourteen months later, on January 27, 2023, after radiation, two clinical trials, three brain surgeries, countless seizures, multiple ambulance rides to the hospital, having received more MRIs, pokes, prods, and ports than should be considered humanly possible, and a parting-gift staph infection contracted during one of the surgeries, Chris was sent home to die. Or, as it was presented to the family, sent home under hospice care armed with all of the pharmaceuticals to keep him comfortable since life saving options were no longer an option. At this point, he was confined to a wheelchair with paralysis to the left side of his body. The cancer was the least of his problems; the staph infection and rampant inflammation were vying for what was left of him. They were determined he'd make it one, maybe two more months at best.

Stunned, reeling, surreal, numb. We'd known the inevitable outcome from the moment of diagnosis, yet those statistics were for other people. Not in a superior way. In a way filtered through disbelief and denial, sprinkled with hope and determination. The other people must not have had the meal train signups, the carpools, the friends, neighbors, family, access to the top medical communities and surgeons, the medical insurance, a young son and daughter to live for, the right attitude or mindset. Surely our clan had calibrated the correct combination necessary to make this survivable.

We all continued to rally around Chris with our own mix of protocols that included sheer will and determination, a trip back to Disney, some Vietnamese voodoo, a prayer vigilante, obscure energy work practices, Herculean efforts made with big-wheeled beach chairs to dip his toes in the beloved surf, and countless visits made by countless loved ones from near and far. We threw everything we had at cancer, and cancer threw everything it had at Chris.

On November 1, 2023, surrounded by loved ones ... how many times have I read those words, "surrounded by loved ones"? What does that even mean? What does it look like? What does it sound like? What does it feel like in the room at the actual moment when these other people are surrounded by loved ones?

I now understand that surrounded by love is the greatest gift you can give. I thought birthing someone into the world was exceptional, and it is. I just wasn't prepared for the incomprehensible beauty with which human beings can hold the space for another to leave this world. It was the most extraordinary experience of my existence thus far.

On November 1, 2023, Chris Reid, our son, brother, husband, father, uncle, grandson, friend, neighbor, coworker, patient passed peacefully surrounded by loved ones, ending his battle with cancer. And we all began our new journey as other people who survive without him.

# Luau Crasher

## Tonya Reid

Sitting at a luau with one of my besties, I get a tap on the back of my cortex. I ignored it at first, or maybe I didn't quite notice it. Maybe I am just too close to the fire twirlers, or the rhythm of the beating drums has taken over the cadence of the blood pumping through my skull, or more than likely, I am getting a brain freeze from my frozen fruity concoction that came with the buffet I am about to chow down on.

Oh, there it is again. It feels like a tiny tap on my shoulder. The one you get while standing in line, not paying attention, and the person behind you ever so slightly takes their index finger and lightly raps on your back to make you aware that it's your turn to move along. Only there's no line, there's no one behind you, and there's nowhere to move along to, or so you think.

I am in Maui visiting my girlfriend Sharon. I met her years earlier in Charlotte, North Carolina, where I live and she grew up. I met her on one of her home base visits. I call them that because, at one time, Charlotte was her home, and she always boomerangs back home to Charlotte, yet it never really feels quite like home to her anymore. It's become more of her reset place. The place she can come and know her way around while she's proverbially finding her way around. A way station until her journey takes her somewhere else.

Sharon and I are the kind of friends that can say to each other, "Hey! I need to grab this other call. Can I get right back to you?" And "get right back to you" can turn into six months, five time zones, or forty-six hundred miles away. We pick right back up mid-sentence. No harm, no foul.

Being the consummate hostess, she would have been remiss to send me back to the mainland without me experiencing this Hawaiian tradition. As we are perched in paradise being plied with platters of poi and poke and pork, surrounded by honeymooners and ukulele crooners, my invisible visitor is getting impatient. This time, I scan the crowd, and my eyes land on a couple a few tables over. Goosebumps start making the hairs on my arms and the back of my neck stand up. *Ugh! Not now*, I think, and I go back to stuffing my belly, hoping this messenger will move along.

Nope. Now this disembodied delegate from beyond is starting to be a nag and a major distraction from dinner and the show. Try as I may, my attention keeps getting drawn to that couple. The best way I can describe it is the feeling you get when you are all snug in your bed, lights out, your pillow is perfectly positioned under your head, you are totally relaxed, drifting off into the ethers, and suddenly, out of nowhere, completely uninvited to the slumber party, you get the faintest inkling from deep in the recesses of your psyche that you may have left the stovetop on or the door unlocked. And you know that sensation is just going to get more and more intense until you get up and do something about it. There goes your bedtime bliss. It is the absolute worst, right?!

I turn to Sharon, who is starting to notice my rubbernecking, and I blurt out, "I have a message for the guy at that table! There's something I have to tell him!"

Being my mystical soul sista, she doesn't bat an eye and responds with, "Then go tell him."

"Noooooo! I can't!" I retort. "The message is for him, not her. I can't tell him with her around."

I go back to our feast wishfully thinking that the courier from beyond would be satisfied that I had, at the very least, acknowledged their presence out loud. Feeling some relief, I turn my attention to what's going on at my own table and put it out of my mind, knowing that my hands are tied because it is very clear to me that I cannot tell the dude what I need to tell him as long as he is around his companion.

Better luck next time, specter! Sucka! Look at me getting off on your technicality!

I settle into our surroundings. Enjoying the ocean breeze. Drinking it all in. The performers are amazing. I have never seen so many stars in the sky. The foliage and the grounds are indescribable. Lush on steroids! Ahhhh, this is living.

After a while, I excuse myself to go find the restroom. I was concentrating so intently on navigating the stepping stones winding around the dimly lit path to the privy that I didn't notice that there was someone, an actual someone, like with an actual body and all, headed directly my way. I look up, and I am face to face with the intended recipient of my metaphysical communiqué. It is the guy that the unseen has been bugging the ever living shit out of me all night to go talk to, AND he is ALONE!

We both are momentarily caught off guard on this single lane walkway. I think, *Here goes nothing!*

The words start stumbling out of my mouth, "You're—you're going to think I'm crazy, but I have a message for you from Spirit."

This khaki pants, loafer, no sock wearing, straight-laced, banker/lawyerish looking dude looks straight at me with eyes wide and says with confusion, "Okay."

Not sure how long this deer caught in headlights of a man is going to be amenable to this download I'm receiving, the words begin tumbling out of my mouth as if punctuation didn't exist, "Please don't think I'm crazy but I have a message for you from Spirit that's what I call it anyway you can call it whatever you want to I don't know anything about you or the lady you are with or anything about your situation I just know that you had a choice to make does this make any sense to you?"

He stood there dumbfounded, holding his breath, nodding his head, without blinking.

I elaborated, "Okay. Good. Well, I'm supposed to tell you that you had a choice to make. And you need to know that you made the right decision."

This guy let out the biggest sigh of relief, and he looked like the weight of the world had been lifted off of his shoulders.

I implored, "So you know what I'm talking about? You don't have to give me any details. It's just really important that you know you made the right choice."

He responded, "Yes, I know exactly what you're talking about, and thank you."

I smiled, wished him luck, and we each went on our way. I had absolutely NO IDEA what options that man was faced with. Was he supposed to get married, thought he was in love with someone else, went through with the ceremony anyway out of a sense of obligation, and now they were on their honeymoon? Was he a runaway groom leaving his bride at the altar, now on this romantic getaway with some little presumed tartlet that's actually the love of his life? Did his parents or her parents not approve of their union but love won?

By the time I got back to the table, the couple was gone. I was left with far more unknowns than certainties. Hopefully, Mr. Man was now enjoying his evening and his future with more knowns than uncertainties. All I knew for sure was that I was going to check my bill and confirm that I wasn't charged for the three-wheeling wisp that had attached itself to our party of two!

---

TONYA REID is a hairdresser by trade and the author of *US Hairways: Snippets from a Hairdresser's Journey.* She has always had a knack for entertaining and storytelling behind the chair. After raising her blended family of four boys with her husband, Billy Reid, and stepping away from her bustling hair salon, she is enjoying having a damn minute to herself to get those thoughts on paper. Being off-the-charts extroverted and passionate about supporting others' dreams, she is a powerful speaker and consultant. She is the author of. Connect with Tonya on Instagram @thetonyareid.

# Free to Be Me

## Kristin Bowen

I had spent years working on myself. I did everything from yoga, diet, and exercise to traditional therapy, hypnotherapy, moms' groups, breathing exercises, plant medicine, and more. As soon as she said the words, my face twisted with shock and confusion. I was offended. "He is the best thing to ever happen to you," my grandmother explained with excitement and pride as she shared her inner thoughts about the impact my husband had made on my life.

What did she even mean? What about my growth? What about all I'd done to get to this place of peace? I'd worked my ass off to be this cool, calm, and collected. Did she not notice the work I had been doing all this time? In my head, I paused. All those years of trauma and, yes, tons of healing, but I still had a victim mentality. I couldn't help but feel sorry for myself. At that moment I realized I had not yet made it to my final destination of healing. Is there even such a thing as "the end" of healing? Clearly, I still had soul searching and work to do on myself, and this journey wasn't quite over yet.

That wasn't the first time I had heard a comment like that. Usually people would word it as how lucky I am to have him in my life. They would go on and on about his good qualities, captivating smile, ability to be patient amidst our daily chaos, and stellar problem-solving abilities.

See, now I've come to realize that two truths can exist at once. He certainly is one of the best things to happen to me. But it's also true that because of my work and personal discovery, I was able to accept him into my life. Our relationship has stood the test of time, stress, challenges, and imperfections along with a daily dash of joy, grace, and laughter. We have gone through hell and back together and are now even closer than either of us could have imagined. Our bond has become unbreakable. Clearly, others could see the joy and peace that I had found in my life, and my grandmother was simply calling out the obvious. So why did it feel like a smack in the face or a punch in the gut?

In the early years of our relationship, I didn't trust him. Hell, I didn't trust anybody. I thought I had to do it all, and I refused to accept any help. You know the drill. You've probably seen it before. I would stack all ten grocery bags along my arms while toting a kid on one hip and pushing a stroller on the other. I cooked dinner, did bath time, and put all the kids to bed after a long day of work, while protesting any help that was offered. It felt like my job to solve everyone else's problems, while screaming on the inside.

About three years into our relationship, I was utterly frustrated. I'd had enough of the rat race and wanted to get out. I could no longer keep the screaming on the inside and wanted to rip my hair out because I felt so alone in my own mess. I watched him regularly sit on the couch and relax after dinner. He would unwind by watching TV, playing games on his phone, or hanging out with the kids. I would clean the kitchen, making sure every dish, counter, and appliance was clean. On this particular night, he asked me to come sit with him. I yelled back, "I can't! All of these dishes need to get done, and it has to be clean before I can even think of relaxing!" He looked shocked and surprised. He certainly wasn't expecting that reaction. In that moment, he stared at me with the most caring eyes, and I could tell he could see right through my pain. He knew how bitter I felt about him sitting while I did all the work. Slowly and with a clear, firm voice, so that I knew he was serious, he said one of the most honest statements I've ever heard, "You can sit down too, you know? We can do the dishes later." That "we" meant everything. To this day, I'm still not sure he realizes how much that moment impacted our lives.

My brain was instantly rewired. Something clicked at that moment. Suddenly, I didn't have to hold up this perfect persona. I didn't have to do everything, and I certainly didn't have to do it alone. Yes, he is a nice guy and was offering to split the household chores, cooking, cleaning, and taking care of the kids. This wasn't the "aha" moment. He was always nice. He always offered to help when I needed it. The moment it all came together was my realization that I could also relax whenever the hell I wanted to—dishes done or not. My needs, wants, and personal desires were important too.

The things is, he had always been true to himself and his own needs—taking a nap when he needed it, eating the candy, ice cream, or cake because he felt like it, not going to a "mandatory" social event or kid's birthday party simply because he didn't feel like it, and, yes, sitting on the couch after dinner to enjoy some time to himself before cleaning up the kitchen. See, the thing is, he didn't change himself to accommodate my beliefs, emotions, or needs. He also wasn't avoiding the work or expecting me to do it all. I had made up in my head all of these stories and expectations for myself. He was simply true to himself and what he desired. In that moment he forever changed how I view my own needs. I now know how to give myself permission to do what I want, and I'm so thankful that he was able to voice this permission to me so that I no longer needed to question my own wants and desires.

I do consider myself lucky now, and I also think each of us has the ability within ourselves to create this "luck." My husband is the type of guy who lights up the room when he walks in. Everyone tells him the party starts when he arrives. This bothers him, or maybe it just confuses him, mostly because he doesn't think he is doing anything special. He doesn't want extra credit or a trophy. He is just being himself. This is part of what makes it so magical. It just happens naturally. This is how he lives his life.

I sit back and analyze all of this for a while, watching him in awe as he unapologetically takes up space and moves throughout this world like he owns it, all rightfully so! My not so scientific conclusions tell me he doesn't do anything special or "over the top." He is, however, unique. Unique in his ability to be fully himself at all times, no matter the person or place he is standing in front of at any given time. He doesn't put on a "mask" or try to fit in. He doesn't hold back or hold his tongue. He is big and bold and beautiful, and perhaps, to others, he is loud and annoying or maybe even rude and unkind. As I observe, this tends to be the best part. He is unbothered by others' feelings about who he is at his core because his intent is always pure and kind. It's not about them. He isn't acting a certain way to please others or to make them like him. None of that matters. It's astounding to watch someone walk in their own shoes with such confidence and understanding about themselves. He doesn't question himself or stutter over his thoughts and beliefs. There are no "what if" or "do you think they like me" questions.

He lights up the room because people love his energy and presence. The real kicker is, the thing they like about him the most and don't even realize is that he gives them permission to be totally free and embrace who they are as well. His presence alone gives each of us the ability to be free—free of judgment, free of questions about our beliefs, free of negativity or rejection, and free from limiting beliefs that hold us back. This has truly been the biggest gift he has brought to my life. He brought himself. He brought the lesson for me to learn the art of being me. So, yeah, he is the best thing to happen to me.

Those that we feel most comfortable around and want to spend our time with are often the ones who make us feel as though we are at home, as though we belong. This home actually lives within us. The most distinguished quality of these individuals is that they let us fully be ourselves, without apology or hesitation. They accept us for who we are on our best days and even on our worst. What is unique about these folks is that they not only hold the space for us to be ourselves, but also are utterly and completely vulnerable with us by showing who they truly are at all times. It is not the acceptance given to us but the acceptance that others have of themselves that allows us to accept the deepest and darkest parts of our authentic selves too.

I've come to realize that the secret to not caring what others think rests on the fact that I would rather be disliked for who I am than to be liked for being somebody that I am not. So take the nap, skip the party, wear mismatched clothes, and snort while you laugh, simply because it's what you enjoy. You'll soon realize that anyone who has a problem with how you act or who you are probably has a real problem with themselves. On the outside, they may be poking fun or giving you the side eye or even judging you for being yourself, yet on the inside, they are full of guilt and shame for not being as bold and free as you are to embrace who they are at their core.

To my grandmother and anyone else who thinks my husband is the best thing that ever happened to me, you are right. I couldn't have asked for a more loving, supportive, and kind partner to walk by my side every day. I also think you don't need to have a husband or life partner to be lucky. The real luck comes from doing the work on ourselves every day so that we can welcome and accept the people, just like my husband, who are here to remind us how amazing we are, because truly, we are the best things to ever happen to ourselves. Again, both things can be true.

# Depression

## Kristin Bowen

She said she didn't want to be here anymore. Well, that's not what she said. That's what I heard.

She was curious about what it would be like or how others would feel if she wasn't here any longer.

My heart was ready to burst. All I could feel were aches and pains, a desperate longing for a slow, deep breath. I had felt this type of pain before, but this time it was different. I imagined a knife had just pierced the center of my soul. It may have broken my heart in half that day.

I feared this day would come for at least one of my children. With a long line of depression and mental illness in my family, it seemed almost inevitable that my own childhood experiences and bouts of depression would play a part in helping my children one day.

In a family of six, we don't get a lot of one-on-one time together, and here we were, just the two of us, sitting at the dining room table with fewer distractions than usual. We were both eating a snack while the rest of the house was buzzing with the normal activity, TV on in the background, dogs barking outside, and the other kids settling into the living room after school. This felt like a special moment, precious alone time together, yet all of that changed in a split second.

Haley seemed to survey the room, seeing who was home, if anyone paying attention, and who was within earshot of her voice. She glanced over at me to give the heads up that she wanted to tell me something later. It was the way she looked at me. I felt like I could read her mind. This information was intended just for me, "not Daddy." She knows, in our family, we don't keep secrets, and clearly, I was going to share the information with her dad, but she needed to tell me in confidence, alone. Immediately, my body went into fear mode. I was on high alert, and my ears were perked. I was not a fan of waiting, and the way in which she presented this information, it felt urgent. She had already been telling me, and showing me, for weeks how she was extremely sad, stressed, and often felt like she couldn't control her emotions. All of this made her even more anxious and unsure because her feelings didn't seem to make sense to her.

I tried to stay calm, using every tool in my arsenal. I'm not sure if I did a good job of masking my panic or not, but I didn't want her to realize the fear that my body was experiencing. I quickly slapped on a soft smile, squinted my eyes to hide the tears swelling up, smashed my big feelings deep down into my belly, and asked her, "What is it, honey? What did you want to share?" I was trying to be open-minded and make sure she knew I could handle anything she was going to throw at me, but I wasn't even sure I could handle what she was about to say.

She didn't sugarcoat it and downplay what she had to say—or perhaps she didn't realize the weight of what she was going to share. She's given me permission to share this story and her words because she now understands the importance of saying these things out loud and sharing with others who may be experiencing similar feelings.

She told me she was having thoughts of ending it all. She had considered what it would be like to die. "Sometimes it's just too hard,"— life, I imagine—"and I want to give up."

That was the exact moment my heart shattered, or maybe it burst, into a million pieces. I felt a deep, sad longing and hopelessness in a single second. I hope I didn't show it on my face. It was like somebody sucked the literal life, my entire essence, out of my body, so perhaps I was frozen in time without an expression at all. After a pause, I asked her some more questions. I had to be sure I heard her correctly and uncover where all of this was coming from.

I took my mom hat off for a second and had to dig deep, deep down, far below the feelings I had squashed down in my belly earlier, and pull out my box of counseling tools. I had almost two decades of experience at this point; clearly, I should be able to help her process this situation without projecting or making assumptions about why or how she got here. I knew I had to figure out what stage of depression she may be experiencing. Was this a curiosity, suicidal ideation, or had she begun to think of ways to kill herself, how she was actually going to die?

She was so open. I was in awe of her calmness, her bravery, to share these intimate thoughts and scary scenarios with me. She talked about the idea of falling out of a tree or jumping off a bridge. These were all things I too had thought of as a child. I wasn't quite sure what to think of the comparison. Did this mean our thoughts were "normal" and everyone had them, or had I cursed her with a possible lifetime of depression?

As she continued to share, she posed a question. I wasn't sure if she was asking me specifically or wanted to know in general how others would feel. "What would people think if I was gone?" I stayed quiet trying to figure out if I should speak. I began to realize that while it felt like we were alone, the other kids were still moving about the house, and my husband had just come home. "Well," she said, "what would people think if I was gone? Like, how would they feel if I wasn't here anymore?"

My brain couldn't quite comprehend the added heaviness of this question. I felt like a balloon that had been blown up past its breaking point and—pop! I absolutely lost it. All of those feelings I squeezed and compressed into a tiny ball in the pit of my stomach came rushing out of my body and exploded. I instantly became a big, sloppy puddle and melted. All I felt was despair and hopelessness. I had failed, and at the detriment of one of the most precious things in this world. I didn't heal myself quickly enough and felt the guilt of passing these feelings onto her. I had failed her.

How could I box up the amazement, pride, and joy that I felt about her and implant it into her mind, body, and soul? How could I take the immense amount of undeniable and unconditional love I had for her and place it in her hand? I leaned in and put my face as close to her as possible, so she knew how much I meant what I was about to say, and stared at her eye to eye with tear drops ready to make waterfalls down my face. Then I whispered, "My entire world, my most precious thing in the world would be gone. I would be crushed and don't know what I would do with myself. I'm not sure I would be able to go on by myself. I would never be able to forgive myself for allowing that to happen to you and not teaching you how to love yourself the way that I love you so deeply to my core."

My breaths were shaky, and I was sobbing. We held each other so tightly that I thought we may melt into each other. I didn't want to let go of our embrace for fear of the unknown. What happens next? Where do we go from here? I'd had these thoughts before too, and I was never this brave.

In that moment, I was so honored that she trusted me, felt safe enough, had enough space to be vulnerable, knowing that I would have the strength to carry this for her. I knew what I had to do next. Again, I got eye to eye with her, and with the most serious look I could muster through glassy, wet eyes, I made her pinky promise that any time she had these thoughts, she would tell me before ever taking any action. It didn't matter what I was doing, where we were, or if I seemed too busy; she had to know she could come to me again. She promised me, and I reminded her that we don't break promises in this family and that no matter what was going on, I would *always* stop and listen when she needed me.

That moment was intense, and I didn't want her to fear reliving this emotional experience next time she shared these thoughts with me. I knew these feelings all too well. One thing I knew for sure was that she needed to know she wasn't alone. I asked her what she would want to do next time she had these kinds of feelings. I gave her a few of my own personal favorites, knowing that's exactly what I would want to do with someone if I was having these same feelings. "Snuggle up in the back of the car with ice cream? Take a ride in the car with the windows down and music blaring?" She smirked a bit and said, "Yeah, and a little girl chat." She paused for a second. I think she didn't want to hurt my feelings or offend me. "Sometimes I don't want to talk about it at all, okay?" I agreed wholeheartedly. She didn't have to explain herself to me. I know that sometimes you feel these things, and there is no "reason" that you can point to and say what caused this pain. There is nothing to "talk about." I assured her that we never had to talk if she didn't want to, and if she told me how she was feeling, then that was enough.

I still wanted to shake her a little bit and scream out to her that it gets better. If I could have, I would have cut a piece of my heart out and given it to her so she would know the love I have for her every day. I could have jumped into action trying to fix her life and figure out all the things that weren't going well so that we could change them. I was armed and ready to share with her all of my tips and tricks and life hacks for solving my own depression. Thankfully, my experience told me that none of that mattered. I can't fix her problems for her, no matter how hard I try.

I don't think she needed the reminder that day, but I told her anyway: "Whenever you need me to, I'll jump right down in that deep, dark hole and sit with you. I'll be next to you until you are ready to come out, no matter how long it takes."

---

KRISTIN BOWEN, a Delaware native born and raised in Wilmington, invites readers on a transformative exploration of her life. From her early days as a timid child with no voice to becoming the fierce and confident woman she is today, Kristin's journey reflects her commitment to continuous growth and learning combined with the power of unleashing trauma.

Kristin finds immense joy and comfort in her roles as a devoted wife and mother to her four daughters, ranging in age from seven to eighteen. Family holds a central place in her heart, and she cherishes the precious moments spent together.

The writings included in this collaborative work serve as a testament to Kristin's unwavering spirit. Follow her on Instagram @Kjacks99 or on Facebook @Kristinbowen99.

# A Twisted Thank You

## Shana Hartman

Thank you for validating my hunches
For confirming those tingles I used to feel
those knowings where my skin
And heart
And lungs
And throat told me something.was.not.right.

Every move you've made since has been nothing but
affirmation
confirmation
celebration
That I rarely was afforded during.

Now, as you twist and turn another into your web
I am laughing through tears of sadness
Your prey is, well, just that.

"Good luck"
"Safe travels"
"May the force be with you"
come to mind.

Mostly, I send a big shield around the ones I love the most
Hoping, wishing, praying that they find themselves,
Avoid the web, know they are their own
And find their "thank yous" as needed.

# Work Hard, Fail Harder

## Shana Hartman

66 "This isn't what I signed up for. I'd like to leave this program." These are words no business owner likes to hear, yet I have dealt with this a few times in my journey as an entrepreneur. An unhappy client or customer is never the goal for any business. Yet a poor review, an unsatisfied customer, or having to release a client from a program are all a normal part of the life of a business. It's going to happen, but we treat these moments like failures, and, in turn, we treat failures like something to avoid at all costs. In true Carrie Bradshaw, *Sex in the City* fashion, "I couldn't help but wonder," what is the big deal with failing?

## Perfect Oppression

I grew up under the typical Western culture regime and story that my output directly impacted what I received in life. Such stories included the frequent repetition of phrases like …

*Work hard and you'll achieve your goals.*
*You get what you give.*
*Nothing is for free.*
*No pain, no gain.*
*Don't take no for an answer.*
*Failure is not an option.*

I know I'm not the only one who has heard these lines, fed to me like nutritious mantras intended to inspire and motivate me to strive, push, and keep going at all costs. What wasn't included in these well-intentioned stories and quippy one-liners was the historical context that many of them came from: industrial, time-for-money, supremacy-based, oppressive models of what it means to be a productive worker and human. I'm not going to dive into that here, but a bit of quick research will take you far into the root of these ideas and ideals.

Ultimately, the impact of this "you are how hard you work" ideology is a ton of pressure to be perfect and do everything right. Pressure to perform, pressure to be "successful," pressure to avoid failure. And, since I happen to be a female-identifying human, we can tack on an additional layer of pressure to prove myself productive and worthy. For anyone who comes from a marginalized community, the pressure just builds and builds. Again, I ask, but why? Why are we so fascinated with avoiding failure?

It's confusing to operate under these seemingly conflicting understandings: "failure is not an option" and "it's not how many times you fall, but how many times you pick yourself back up." Which is it? Society might tell you both. I say none of it.

## Work Hard, Fail Harder

As I'm writing this, I recently released a client from her program (the one I shared at the start of this piece). We both realized that working together was just not a good fit for a variety of reasons. I took ownership that maybe I had not clearly prepared the client for what to expect and what was included in the program, maybe the client had found something that worked better for them, and maybe we both realized that the energy that would be needed to "work hard" and make this partnership a "success" was higher than what we were willing to give. I shared a video on my social media feed about this experience, and I focused on how we need to normalize losing or releasing clients. Another very kind friend sent me a sweet message of condolence in response. They were very "sorry to hear I lost a client" and wanted to reassure me of my value and worth, wishing me continued success. There it was again—connecting a lack of failures with the promise of success.

I quickly realized in my experience with releasing my client that letting something go, aka failing, should be directly taught to us from a young age. Whether that be not finishing a book, cutting off a toxic relationship, or ending a misaligned business partnership, we should be much more comfortable with failure than most of us are. I mean, we work so hard to teach people how to work so hard. There are courses, books, training, workshops, therapy, tools, and resources all focused on the power of hard work, leaning into something that may feel difficult or uncomfortable. If you have gone to any kind of fitness class, you know exactly what I'm talking about!

And, because of how our culture treats failure, there is often nothing more difficult than admitting "this isn't working." I would argue that failure is just as uncomfortable and difficult as working hard can be, so why not have the courses, books, training, workshops, therapy, tools, and resources focused on navigating the discomfort of failing just like we do for hard work? How would it feel to have been taught, and even encouraged, to fail?

## Succeeding at Failure

In my experience at failure—through my business, my relationships, my parenting, and more—I have learned so much. I learned where my boundaries are and how to readjust them. I have learned how to define and honor my values more clearly. I have learned what I'm willing and unwilling to do to make money, to be in love, to be a good _____ (daughter, sister, mother, friend, woman, etc.). I am succeeding at failing, damn it, and I think more of us should strive to do so as well.

Imagine who you get to be when you release the pressure of not failing. How do you show up for your day? For your family? For yourself? When the goal is no longer perfection, but rather practice. When the pressure to prove something lessens and the hard work of just being and trusting that you are doing your best with what you know right now increases. What is possible when you allow yourself to work hard and fail harder?

SHANA HARTMAN is a former university English professor turned embodied writing coach. She helps heart-centered professionals and thought leaders share the core messages from their life and career experiences in powerful books by using an embodied writing approach that allows people to truly experience their transformative words. She is a published author and founder and CEO of Synergy  Publishing Group. As an ICF certified coach and BodyMind Method© Coach, Shana supports folks in connecting with their inner truth and writing from that place.

Learn more about Shana and the books her clients publish at synergypublishinggroup.com and follow her on Instagram @theshana_v.

# Aching

## Taylor Edwards

I couldn't tell you how many trees surround my home.
They're everywhere.
Standing regal and consistent beside one another, tall, sturdy blades of big grass that hold their ground.

*They are rooted, and they flow.*

Their rigidity, I can relate to, occupying their space in a way that will not budge.

*Ever present, ever unchanging.*

Their fluidity, I grapple with, allowing the breeze to squeeze between each leaf and *wiggle and move* with the wind.

*Malleable and discerning,*

Why trap in amber branches that desire to play?

*I am rooted and I [ache to] flow.*

# Trust

---

## Taylor Edwards

---

Da-dum. Da-dum. Da-duh, da-duh.
Dum.
Dum.
Dum.

I marvel most days
To be both in and of the Universe.

Looking at you, I see eons splayed over your face.
Every pore of your skin is both a supernova and an earthquake.
Combusting, releasing
Producing, devastating.

You are made of stuff much stronger than consciousness
can comprehend.

Your eyes beg of me to answer that which stays on the tip of your
seafoam-pressed tongue:
*What in the world do I do next?*

In the Universe, you sit on bones that are built upon both calamity
and miracle.

Of the Universe, you are disaster and disaster's Divine.

What in the world do you do next?
My dear.
*Whatever the fuck you want.*

# Today

---

## Taylor Edwards

---

Today, I'm going to be happy.
Today, I'm going to be well.
Today, I'm going to trust myself.

*You trust you, you love you, you're kind to you.*

Isn't it a funny thing that I have to fill myself up with these platitudes?
To have a chance of making it through the day.

I don't think we were meant to live this way.

When I asked myself what to do with myself,
A voice inside whispered,
*"You are your fiercest protector."*

"What am I to protect?"
I scream back.

How am I supposed to go about my life
When I'm cursed with the knowing that nothing is right?

The bodies and the bombs and the economy and the fucking election.

My skin crawls when I try to be.

I'll try to turn myself inward.

*You trust you, you love you, you're kind to you.*

Gripping hard onto those words like they're documents that free me.

A fierce protector can be a voice that booms, a roar as you rise.
And it can be a soft turn,
A gentle start,
A simple sentence.

"What am I to protect?"
I ask again, slowly.

A reply: *"Your trust, your love, your kindness."*

In a pregnant moment, clarity buds and Today blooms.

# Discourse

---

## Taylor Edwards

---

You invited me into a new language,
  One I'd never heard before,
And now mastered, since.

Syllables rolled around my mouth
Exploding in stars and color,
No space for connotation,
Our *lex*icon is my safe haven.

An isolate parlance,
Our lingo-morphistic love
Lives in the palette.

Flat full tongue,
Caresses the back of your teeth,
I moved in as we spoke oaths.

I crossed your heart, hope to die,
If ever linguicide.

TAYLOR EDWARDS is a professional manager who believes in the power of words. She lovingly provides structure and organization around the creative magic that is Synergy Publishing Group's Embodied Writing Experience. A writer, reader, and lifelong learner, Taylor spends her time sponging up new information, writing all she can, and spoiling her two purr-fect cats. Connect with her by following her blog, housed at mytaylored.life.

# Nips, Tucks, and Kiss My Butt:

## Embracing Age

---

### Karen Taylor

---

From birth, women are saddled with cultural expectations of beauty and body image heavier than the packs on burros transporting coffee beans. We are expected to fit into the social standards regulating body size. This includes both the overall shape as well as specifics on how big our breasts are and how shapely but not too big our butts are. We are also expected to sport tiny waists and toned hips and thighs, display long, shiny, smooth hair, don the latest stylish clothing, which should be sexy but not slutty, with the same rule applying to makeup, which must be tasteful and not overdone. Other regulations involve the volume of our voices, how we use our words, the topics we choose to discuss, and what professions we choose to pursue.

These standards are not new. They have been around in one form or another for a very long time. This is not the place for a history lesson, but suffice it to say that women's fashion has been the object of a great deal of restriction, mostly by men in power, and not infrequently by men in power in religion.

Because of people living longer, beauty standards for aging have evolved over time as well. Though traditionally women have suffered from looking in the mirror and seeing new wrinkles, sagging skin, and other effects of gravity and living life, these days more and more products are hitting the market labeled as "anti-aging," along with advertisements for Botox injections, plastic surgery, and the like. What if we just addressed the fact that each age we reach should be celebrated for what it is: another year of living, breathing, and enjoying life?

Babies are accepted as beautiful, usually. If a person says a baby is ugly, then they have more issues than an essay about aging and beauty can address. When a baby is born, they represent the beauty of life beginning, but somewhere along the way, that acceptance gets lost in a myriad of cultural bullshit that affects the child's self-esteem, making them forget that they are a beautiful representation of creation.

As the child grows and reaches puberty, they find it is rife with bodily changes that throw them into a tailspin. All of the hormonal changes and navigating societal expectations further buries that original feeling of love and acceptance a baby is given. After navigating puberty, young adulthood comes along, and things level out a little, but the pressure of acceptance from cultural beauty standards doesn't diminish.

Much later in our lives, we are once again thrown into a frenetic whirlwind of hormonal tornado activity with the onset of perimenopause culminating in menopause. This life change is arguably worse than puberty because it brings with it the process of aging and the effects gravity brings on our bodies, which many of us have spent a lifetime already trying to change.

The journey from girl to woman is fraught with skewed opinions of the perfect feminine figure, even down to the actual numbers on a measuring tape. For example, at one time in history, my girlhood, I remember that 36-24-36, was discussed as the ideal feminine shape. Those numbers have changed over time, and I don't know what would be considered "perfect" in that specific group of folks who know or set those numbers, but the underlying message here is the same: expectations for a specific body image for the "perfect female shape" have been in place for a long time, and it is ridiculously stupid.

The cosmetic industry, including plastic surgery, has benefited from one-size-fits-all expectations for a while, but I suspect it is most likely at an all-time high due to the rise of social media sites and the tendency for influencers to post only fantasy-inducing content that further drives girls and women—those not falling into the cookie cutter body image set forth by the patriarchy—to butt lifts, tummy tucks, and Botox. Frequently, anti-aging products pop up on my Facebook and Instagram feeds. Special shampoo and conditioner for gray hair, makeup for "mature" women, special creams for sagging upper arms, and the list goes on, feeding those fears of aging and becoming unattractive.

Things look even bleaker for women who spent their entire lives placing their whole self-worth upon their looks. It is sad for women who spend their lives attempting to attain some unreachable image of themselves that is not based upon authenticity. Our worth is not dependent upon our looks, our sizes, whether or not we have smooth, flowing hair, pouty lips, or tight asses and big breasts. Our worth is based upon so much more than that, and if we don't learn that before we get into our late forties, we will be miserable human beings.

When I hit my fifties, I think I spent almost the entirety of that decade being somewhat depressed about my age. I am not sure at what point I began to make progress in accepting myself, but I finally did. Maybe it was just my logical brain saying, "Well, you might as well just shut the hell up and accept it because what can you do about it?" Or maybe the inner work I had been doing on myself started to help. Regardless of which, I have finally found a place I am much more comfortable, and even though there are days when I still look at myself in the mirror and sigh or see my pudgy middle and remember a fitter physique, for the most part, I accept myself and remind that monster bitch in my head that I am who I am, and I am good.

I heard the phrase "age is freeing" from an older lady in a class I was taking once, and now I am the older lady. I understand what she meant, but of course it is an attitude. I have to remind myself that a lot of freedom does come with aging, and I think that freedom was purchased with years of struggling in life's various venues, trying to be a good daughter, mom, wife, and good at making a living, and all of the other parcels of our lives we carry each day.

After the children were grown, and in my case the death of my spouse, I began looking at things differently, and I have found that the best way to look at aging is that I have another day to spend here on Earth doing my thing, and that is the best it can get, I think.

My grandmother, who is one of my heroes, God rest her soul, never wore makeup a day in her life. Of course, she was born in 1905 in the Bible Belt of the South, so there were many factors that influenced her not wearing makeup. She was petite, pretty, and raised to follow all of those stupid regulations set forth by the combined efforts of religion and the patriarchy, so a big gap existed between her environment growing up and mine, even though my mom was pretty strict about clothing and how much makeup was acceptable.

Whether women choose to wear makeup, certain types of clothing, high-heeled shoes, thigh-high boots, short or long skirts, cut or color their hair, or whatever, should be a decision based upon personal preference for women and not based on any standard set by anyone outside themselves. Aging should be honored, so when we make it another decade, we acknowledge the accomplishments that were achieved. Body shape, size, the volume of a woman's voice, how many wrinkles she has, whether or not her upper arms flap or her butt jiggles, should not even be a consideration concerning who that woman is in the world.

We are human beings, and as such, we should be recognized and valued for that and that alone, not objectified by some stupid image set forth by society. Once we all realize this and use it as our standard, women will be able to become what we deserve to be: respected individuals with hopes, dreams, purposes, and lives to be lived to the fullest. So, yeah, the beauty industry and those who uphold their inhumane standards can take their Botox, their anti-aging remedies, their plastic surgery, and their judgments on a trip, and buy a pair of athletic shoes so they can get a good jump on kissing my butt.

KAREN TAYLOR is a proud mother of a fine young man who served in the Marine Corps, and she is a dog lover to the point of ridiculousness. She loves reading books, spending time with her dogs, and basically being inappropriate. She is an English instructor at a community college in North Carolina and well known for being blunt yet fiercely loyal to family, friends, students, and anyone who is a victim of a bully. Check out Karen's other books and writings *Learning to Respect My Strut: My Journey as a Woman Warrior* (2023), *Unveiling the Secrets: An Encyclopedia by Women, for Women (and Those Who Love Them)* (2023), and *Capturing the In-Between* (2022). Connect with her on Instagram @_karen_taylor.

# Perspective: A Love Note to My Younger, Current, and Future Self

## Charlene Hill

First, to young Charlene, hi, hello, and I love you ... all of you! I want you to know that you had many ups and downs in your life. You have learned to embrace it all! Life is so many things. It is messy. It is stressful. It can be overwhelming. But it is also wonderful, beautiful, and fun.

You have had moments of joy, moments of confusion, and moments of heartbreak. There will be times when you don't understand who you are, where you're going, or what to do with your life, and there will be days when you feel like giving up or running away, but I promise, as you move through your life, you will develop a deeper understanding and connection to who you are, and this will help guide you forward in everything you do.

Know that when you are faced with the toughest of times, you will come out on the other side. Each of these experiences will teach you more and more about yourself. There will be more clarity in your intuition (those feelings you get in your belly!) and your steps, even though you may not see the end results of where you're going. You will feel very supported and guided on your journey because you learn to trust who you are, trust the universe, and trust your intuition.

As you get older, you will live enough years to give you a perspective that you, young Charlene, currently do not have and cannot imagine. With this perspective, you will be able to see the cycles and patterns of life and see how each time you surrender and each time you follow your inner guidance, and intuition, everything always works out for your best and highest good with an unexplainable grace and ease. You will also see the cycles and patterns of what happens when you try to fit into someone else's box or into what society says a woman should do or be or what your daily life should look like and include. You will see how that creates a ripple effect of discomfort mentally and physically and how it creates a disconnect in who you are and how you function in your life, in your relationships, and in the world. There are ways you already see this in your life now. Remember how very early in elementary school you learned that standing and moving is not okay? And that you are wrong and bad for doing what comes naturally to you, like moving? And just how confusing all of that was? You had to be quiet, do as they said, and sit when they said sit, even though you enjoy standing and moving to do your school work in class so that you can process what you are learning and doing. Following these rules resulted in you becoming more and more physically and mentally uncomfortable. You slowly disconnected from who you are and how you function best, and it became harder to focus in classes. As time passes, you will slowly begin to criticize yourself, and by high school, you will have lost some of the weird and quirky traits that make you *you*, and you will have lost the ability to speak up and use your unique voice in writing or creating art in a way that is you, out of fear of doing it wrong or getting a bad grade. This will manifest itself in a number of physical ways ... anxiety, stomach issues, body pain/tension, and headaches. These physical symptoms and the connection to trying to conform are not seen or understood at the time and are something that you will be able to see and acknowledge a decade or so later when you look back through the eyes of perspective and you have moved through some of your self-healing. You do well in school, but it is hard work, and you will come out of high school thinking you are stupid, but believe me, Charlene, you are far from it. You process and learn differently than the way they teach in school, and that is okay.

## A Note to Myself Now

You found your voice as you learned to let go and be more and more yourself over the years, and you discovered better ways of communicating with yourself and with others. You even expanded your art and creative side into writing and publishing ... something that seemed impossible to you since spelling, grammar, and punctuation continues to perplex you into your adult years. You got to the point where you were done living in fear, and you chose to do things for you when you feel that inner pull to take action.

Now, you are focused and intelligent in the things that interest you, and one of the joys of adulthood is the freedom to learn and explore what you love in ways that work for you. You now know how to tune in to you, which actually becomes a powerful entity in your life (congrats on creating TUNE IN 2 YOU®). You now understand the power of self-awareness, self-care, and self-love. For you, it is the feeling of inner peace and being present in the moment and consciously choosing how you would like to feel and how you want to respond. It is the core of who you are and *your* form of spirituality, and it connects all aspects of you back to yourself where you feel whole: body, mind, soul, and energy system.

You learned how to respond rather than react because, as an adult, you consciously continued to learn, grow, and develop what honoring you looks like, feels like, and includes. By taking the time to play, experiment, learn, paint, draw, and color outside all the lines, you found your way back home to you. On this journey, you found and explored many resources, tools, and techniques that helped you deepen your connection to your inner guidance and intuition. You will keep what works for you, coming back to them over and over again, and let go of the rest.

The inner work of art will play a big part in developing your self-awareness and self-love. As you explore and play with your art, it will change you. You already know that it is not always about the end product, it is about the process, the feeling, and the energy of joy and creativity.

The deep connection and feeling you have with your creativity will bring you back to your art over and over again at all ages and stages of life. The memory of the feeling and experience of love and joy in the process of creativity will call you back to it. You fully enjoy that joy now, but there will be times along the way where that gets lost, and you will become more critical of your art and yourself.

There will be times when you doubt the value of your art and yourself. There will be times when you will have moments of despair, depression, and physical pain, and you will pull out your paints and play for the sake of play, for color, and flow. There will be times when, while you are deep in the moment and connected to the journey and the process of creation, all the pain, tension, and depression will just melt away, and you are just you with no judgments, no expectations, no shoulds, and you feel light; you will feel comfortable both in body and mind.

It surprises you the first few times you experience this. It will be as if you swallowed some sort of magic rainbow unicorn pill. This will change you, and over time, with practice, it will be easier and easier for you to allow yourself to connect to the space between your thoughts and words where creativity lives. That comfortable place that you feel not only in memory but also in every cell of your body. From this space, you will create pieces you love and hang on your wall or sell for others to enjoy. And you will create pieces that do not turn out, but that you still love because they served you, your healing, and your connection. This is the healing power of art, not only for you but for those who love your art and purchase it to hang on their walls. What you created holds the energy of that which you created it from.

## A Note to the Whole of You, Young, Current, and Future

Now go have some fun—create, doodle, draw, go outside and chase the bugs, or catch a turtle. Learn that those moments where you are in nature will be a guidepost for you. You feel at home in nature, and you feel at one with who you are. In nature, everything is okay, and your mind is free from self-judgment and worries. You are present as you feel the wind on your face, watch the leaves blow in the wind, watch the water bugs move on the surface of the pond, and hear the nighttime noises through your open window in the spring. As an adult, this is still your favorite sound. Nature is as healing for you as your self-care and your art, and nature has the power in those moments of disconnection and confusion to bring you back into alignment with you and your goals.

Life is a journey, and you are never going to be done growing, evolving, and expanding. As I write this, I realize that I am really writing a love note to all versions of myself throughout my ongoing journey. Young me, the version of me who is writing this now, me in ten to twenty or more years from now. Because no matter what age, these words will help, inspire, uplift, and remind you that there is only one you. So go be the *youest* you can be!

I want you to know you are imperfectly perfect just as you are!

I want you to know that you are an artist.

Know that you are a gift to this world and that you are stronger and capable of more than you can imagine.

You are unique, you are special, and you matter.

Love,
*You*

---

Artist, author, and coach, CHARLENE HILL is dedicated to her own inner work and truly lives the work she puts into the world. The TUNE IN 2 YOU® process that Charlene created is a combination of practical experiments, tools, techniques, and strategies that can help you discover your own UNIQUE way of connecting to your body, mind, and soul so that you  can experience more inner peace, clarity, and joy in your everyday life and as you take intuitively guided action steps toward the life and goals you choose both personally and professionally. When she is not working with clients or writing, you will find her in her art room getting messy as she plays with her paints or meditating outside on her yoga mat, soaking up the sunshine with her fur baby, Sadie. To learn more about Charlene and her work, you can find her at charlenehill.com or on Facebook at Charlene Hill, Inc.

# *An Invitation:*
# It's Your Turn to Spread Some Faerie Dust

## Shana Hartman

In the last season of the hit television series *Sex and the City*, Carrie finds herself dating an artist named Aleksandr Petrovsky, played by the amazing classical dancer Mikhail Baryshnikov. In one scene where Carrie wanders into Aleksandr's art studio to share that she isn't cut out for what she thinks is a temporary, casual-sex kind of relationship, she is pleasantly surprised to discover that there is much more to this man and his work then she had realized.

At the end of the scene, she begins to take in what is really in front of her, noticing the smattering of tools and scraps of this and that he is using to create his latest piece. She then asks, "So what's all this?"

"It's too soon to tell," he replies.

As Cindy and I thought of how we wanted to introduce and conclude this next iteration of *Unveiling the Secrets*, we realized that we, too, have been pleasantly surprised by the "all this" that keeps showing up as we welcome new writers into our embodied writing community. Equally, when we try to define what has been written and where this book series will go, we find ourselves smiling with a knowing of "it's too soon to tell" as well.

See, I have written more words than I could ever count, and I have had the honor of helping even more writers discover and share their own words. Each and every time, my experience begins and ends with this same understanding of what the act of writing gets to be: a constant curiosity and openness to what "all of this" is and a slightly uncomfortable and exciting answer of "it's too soon to tell."

Living in this in-between is where the magic of unveiling and sharing our voices, our stories, our words emerges. *This* is how the faerie dust keeps spreading, like Cindy described at the beginning of the book. We don't have to have answers; we just need to open our hearts and let our hands support what wants to come forward. So, dear reader, it's time for you to explore becoming a "dear writer" as well. Consider the book you are holding as a springing-off point for what faerie dust you might share in our next *Unveiling the Secrets* books. Our writers have touched on the following themes, and I am hoping you have been inspired to join them by submitting a piece of your own. Our next book series themes include, but are not limited to:

- From Surviving to Thriving
- Artistic Endeavors/Creativity
- Body Image
- Aging
- Mental Health
- Relationships
- Trusting Ourselves
- Health Crises and Healing
- Asking Questions More Than Having Answers

Take a moment (yes, right now!) to close your eyes, explore what is showing up, and tune into what you are experiencing as you finish this book. Consider what you are thinking, feeling, noticing, wondering, and so on after reading the words of Melisa, Rachel, Ama, Amanda, Charlene, Fran, Jennifer, Tonya, Kristin, Taylor, Karen, Cindy, and me. Now, take five to ten minutes and do some writing. And look at that—you have just jump-started your submission to be a part of the *Unveiling the Secrets* book series.

Next, head to shanahartman.com/authorsubmissions to finish your submission and potentially join our amazing writing community. We can't wait to add your name to our growing list!

Write on,
*Shana*

# Acknowledgments

There is a false sense that writing a book is a solo act, even when writing a piece of a book. This could not be further from the truth. We want to take a moment to thank those involved in creating something like a collaborative, multi-authored book. First, we continue to thank the authors that keep showing up to share their words:

- Kristin Bowen
- Taylor Edwards
- Melisa Graham
- Amanda Soesbee Kent
- Rachel Patterson
- Karen Taylor
- Tonya Reid

We also want to congratulate and thank our first-time authors in the *Unveiling the Secrets* book series:

- Fran Gardner
- Jennifer Howe
- Ama
- Charlene Hill

Without these amazing writers, we would not be where we are today at Synergy Publishing Group. We would not be able to put these amazing books out into the world, host inspiring workshops and events for other aspiring writers, and truly use writing as a tool for healing our communities.

## To Cindy, from Shana

As always, I am honored and inspired by the work you do! Who knew when we were in our doctoral program, crying and agonizing over the latest research theories and how the hell we were gonna finish our dissertations, that we'd one day be doing this important writing work? Can you believe this is our job? Thank you for all the amazing coaching and writing support you provide our community.

## To Taylor and Melisa, from Cindy and Shana

This team does some kickass work, and it would not happen without the two of you! Taylor, our organization goddess, thank you for making sure we are actually following our carefully thought-out plans and procedures, even when we get excited and want to quick-start something. You help us pause and stay embodied, and we love you for that! Melisa, our publishing production queen, no words can express how amazing your process is for bringing our words to life. You make us look good, literally!

## To Our Readers

We also believe that there are millions of others out there with secrets to share that could improve the world in which we live. Here's the invitation! We hope that you will share your secrets with us by submitting your writing or writing ideas, and adding your own courageous and vulnerable story to our *Unveiling the Secrets* series. Share your submission for potential publication at shanahartman.com/authorsubmissions.

Made in the USA
Middletown, DE
21 September 2024

60816713R00076